S0-BJU-224

# UNDREAMED SHORES

*England's Wasted Empire in America*

Michael Foss

PHOENIX
PRESS

5 UPPER SAINT MARTIN'S LANE
LONDON
WC2H 9EA

A PHOENIX PRESS PAPERBACK

First published in Great Britain
by George G. Harrap & Co. Ltd in 1974
This paperback edition published in 2000
by Phoenix Press,
a division of The Orion Publishing Group Ltd,
Orion House, 5 Upper St Martin's Lane,
London WC2H 9EA

© Michael Foss 1974

The moral right of Michael Foss to be identified as the author
of this work has been asserted by him in accordance with
the Copyright, Designs and Patents Act 1988.

All rights reserved. No part of this publication may be
reproduced, stored in a retrieval system, or transmitted,
in any form or by any means, electronic, mechanical,
photocopying, recording or otherwise, without the prior
permission of the copyright owner and the above
publisher of this book.

This book is sold subject to the condition that it may not
be resold or otherwise issued except in its original binding.

A CIP catalogue record for this book
is available from the British Library.

Printed and bound in Great Britain by
Butler & Tanner Ltd, Frome and London

ISBN 1 84212 077 8

# Contents

1    The Quest                                             9

2    Preparation                                          35

3    Arguments                                            51

4    The Attempt of Captain Thomas Stukeley               67

5    The Attempt of Sir Humphrey Gilbert                  95

6    The Attempt of Sir Walter Raleigh                   133

7    Conclusion                                          175

# Charts

| | *page* |
|---|---|
| The North Atlantic with prevailing currents | 15 |
| The West Indies in the reign of Elizabeth | 122 |
| Voyages to Raleigh's Virginia, 1584–90 | 136 |

# Acknowledgment

I would like to thank my friend Maurice Cochrane for his valuable help with photography and choice of illustrations.

*I*

# I

# The Quest

NO ONE could be unaware, at the land's edge, of the puzzle of the waters. The gulls flying out, the sails following over the horizon interminably suggested the extent of the mystery. The insubstantial movement of mild or calamitous seas besieged the imagination.

The end to mystery begins in the imagination: there all journeys start. To the speculation of the Greek geographers, based on sound science and sounder logic, succeeding ages had added the play of their fantasy, neither scientific nor logical, but reflecting the dreams of men tied to hard country and poor circumstances. The Greek Eratosthenes, in the third century B.C., had calculated the circumference of the earth with fair accuracy. A later Greek, Strabo, agreed with Aristotle that there were inhabited worlds still to be found, at least two continents or even more, 'especially at the latitude of Athens, if the parallel is extended into the Atlantic'. A sea journey to India was thought possible, for though the ocean was huge, a passage could be done 'with a good east wind following'. And soon, into the cautious spaces guessed at by the geographers, the poets dropped the lands of their imaginings. Seneca spoke of an age of discovery in words which Columbus remembered, when 'Ocean will undo the chains of things, and the great world will be revealed, and a new mariner, like Jason's pilot Tethys, will discover a new world so that Thule will not be the farthest land'.

This prophecy was, as an English poet complained, nothing but 'a flash of poetry'; yet poetry guided the spirit of discovery as strongly as the compass. Beyond Thule, the ultimate land of the ancients, were placed the realms of desire. In this map of the mind lay the land of Saint Brendan, 'the fairest country eastward that any man might see, and was so clear and bright that it was an heavenly sight to behold'. There, too, sparkled the Fortunate Isles, 'those *insulae fortunatae*, which are embraced about with waters sweet, redolent, and cristaline: the tears of the vine are not so precious, the nectar of the gods nothing so sweet and delicious'. And there stood the high mountain of the Terrestrial Paradise that Sir John Mandeville spoke of, its summit near the circle of the moon, surrounded by a monstrous wall whose one gate was closed by ever-burning fire. In the aetherial topography of the poet lay the Lost Atlantis, the Floating Islands, Ophir, the kingdom of Prester John. These were the lands of the aching heart, the quiet utopias of ease and peace whose contemplation offered hope to men caught in the sullen and warlike dominions of Europe.

Who would not seek out new discoveries to realize that content? 'If Paradise', wrote Cosmas, a sixth-century monk and geographer, 'were really on the surface of this world, is there not many a man among those who are so keen to learn and search out everything, that would not let himself be deterred from reaching it? When we see that there are men who will penetrate to the ends of the earth in search of silk, and all for the sake of filthy lucre, how can we believe that they would be deterred from seeking Paradise?' The sails of discovery were driven on by boisterous and contrary winds of vision, chance, greed.

Believers in the Earthly Paradise looked for signs to approve their faith. Western experience, they guessed, did not make up the sum of the universe, but they wanted the evidence of history that other fields, other climates more kind to man existed, and in that agreeable air nature might be perfected without the familiar burdens of toil, ambition and disease. In the closing years of the thirteenth century two men talked in a Genoese prison. The one who held forth was a middle-aged Venetian with the impenetrable stare of a Tartar and the memories of twenty-five years' travel in strange parts; his companion, a Tuscan with some literary ability, listened and questioned and wrote things down in an Italianate French. The topics of the queer-looking Venetian were government, and administration, and trade, warfare, travel, science, sorcery. He spoke of cities more than fifty miles in circumference, and of another built on canals crossed by 12,000 bridges; he spoke of metalled roads and waterways that stretched as far as the eye could see, of caravans that took an hour to pass, of postal systems and paper money; he talked of pearl fisheries, about the export of dried pygmies, about warehouses full to the brim of spices. The Tuscan wrote, and in 1298 the *Travels of Marco Polo* was finished. In these circumstantial and detailed pages Europe found the long-awaited signpost to the new life.

Riches and wonders were the ordinary expectations from the east, and other travellers before Marco Polo had brought back fabulous hints for western credulity. Such reports had been easy to disbelieve. 'There is a certain province', a Flemish traveller had written fifty years before Polo, 'on the other side of Cathay, and whatever a man's age when he enters that province, he never gets any older.' This search for eternal youth suddenly seemed possible after Marco Polo. Could not that province 'on the other side of Cathay' be the Cipangu of the *Travels*? Everywhere, in the pages of Polo, there was a reality as strange as fiction that made fiction itself seem unexceptionable. The Great Khan, with his parks and palaces, his sorcerers and servants, his 10,000 falconers, 20,000 huntsmen and infinite herds of white horses, was no less extraordinary than Polo's magician of Mosul, the one-eyed cobbler who moved mountains. The kingdom of Kublai Khan was larger, more powerful, more complex than the west could conceive. Never had such beauties been observed, such riches been counted; gold shone, jewels glittered in the tantalizing pages of Polo so that his countrymen, half in envy, half in wonder, called him *il Milione*. Nor were the treasures of Cathay the end of his revelations. Since miracles happen most easily in places beyond investigation, Polo himself spoke of the ultimate land of wonders to the east of China, the unvisited island of Cipangu, where the people were white and courteous, where the woods breathed perfumes and spices grew like weeds, where roofs and floors were inlaid with gold, and where the dead were buried with a pearl in the mouth. 'It is a rich island,' Polo concluded, 'so rich that none can tell its wealth.'

Within a century the *Travels of Marco Polo* had been copied in over a hundred manuscripts and translated into Latin, Italian, Spanish and German. It became the textbook of Europe's dreams. In the astonishing quarries of Polo was marble for the romancers, which they plundered gratefully, and none more boldly than Sir John Mandeville, the arch-liar of the Middle Ages, whose *Voiage and Travaile* won the popularity so often given to stark impossibility and unbalanced invention. But the ghost of the Venetian haunted others more sober than the romancers; scholars and geographers usually allowed the evidence of Marco Polo to be a part of their calculations. The account of Cathay, and particularly the evocation of the profoundly mysterious Cipangu, set a quest for Europe.

The advance of the Ottoman Turks, which began fifty years after

Polo wrote, overran Constantinople in 1453 and only stopped at the gates of Vienna, had cut off the land route to the east. New ways were sought to reach the Earthly Paradise, which lay, as all agreed, to the far north-east of Asia. The globes, even those of the time with their superfluous shapes and mythical shores, revealed possibilities by water. Desire and curiosity were strong enough, now that the simple land passage was frustrated, to conquer the natural fear of the open sea. Two sea-routes could be observed on the maps. There was the long way east round the coast of Africa, tediously skirting the shore for many thousand miles. And there was what seemed to be a shorter yet more dangerous enterprise, the western plunge into the Atlantic and the unknown beyond.

The western passage had already been made and half forgotten. At the end of the tenth century Leif Erikson and his countrymen had made a northern crossing in a few large steps, from Iceland to Greenland and on to a strange shore, thus avoiding the dread of the vacant ocean spaces. On the newfound coast of America they recorded that they came first to a place of stones, then to a land of timber, and at last to Vinland, the country of the grape where the grass hardly withered and the dew tasted sweet. The settlements of the Norsemen did not endure. Isolation broke up the community as surely as the frost would split the walls of the abandoned houses. The colonies died and only the rumour of their austere history remained. When Vinland appeared on a fifteenth-century map it was an island placed in the north Atlantic, in the barren region of icebergs and sour winds. No one confused it with the Earthly Paradise, or thought that it was the door to the Indies.

Other islands, some imaginary and some real, in the more southerly parts of the Atlantic gave a better hope for the success of an expedition to the west. The map-makers persuasively put the imaginary islands of the Seven Cities, of Antillia and Brasil far out in the Atlantic as if they were at the half-way stage to Cathay. The journeys of the Portuguese sailors, which discovered the Canaries and the Azores in the first part of the fifteenth century, seemed to confirm the maps. An indulgent interpretation of the evidence, a convenient twisting of the ancient geographies, a wilful redrawing of the charts made the distance from the Canaries to Polo's Cipangu seem only 3,000 nautical miles, less than a third of the true distance. By a further piece of self-deception Columbus even reduced this distance so that he expected Cipangu at the longitude of the West Indies and Cathay in the place of Mexico.

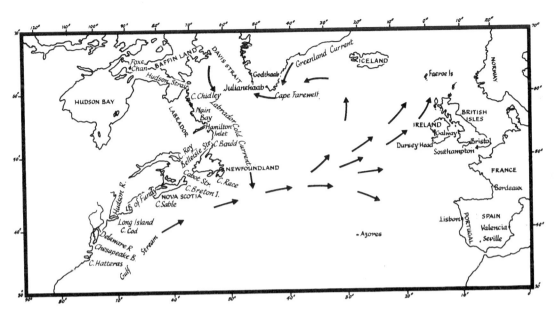

Chart 1   The North Atlantic with prevailing currents.

The true aims of Columbus are made incalculable by the reticence of the past, by his own misconceptions. But it is certain that he hoped to find the way to Cipangu, Cathay and the infinite riches that Polo had described. In the pages of his books, many of which are preserved, he underlined accounts of the rare and valuable commodities. In Pierre d'Ailly's *Imago Mundi* he heard the brazen ring of gold, silver, crystal; in Marco Polo he saw the wink of pearls, rubies, silks, brocades, ivory, and smelt subtle aromas of pepper, cloves, cinnamon, nutmeg. Paolo Toscanelli, the Florentine doctor who in 1474 had first recommended a westward passage to the active mariners of the Portuguese court, had dwelt on the extraordinary wealth of the east. Some ten years later Columbus wrote to the aged Toscanelli for further information, and the old man replied commending 'your noble and grand desire to go to the regions where the spices grow'; such a voyage, he continued, 'will be to powerful kingdoms and cities and provinces, very noble, very rich in all kinds of produce, abundant, of great importance to us; rich in all manner of spices, with precious stones in abundance'. Toscanelli, too, vastly underestimated the distance: treasure awaited, time was flying, advantages such as never existed before might be won by any western prince. Columbus knew: 'gold', he wrote, 'is the most precious of all commodities; gold constitutes

15

treasure, and he who possesses it has all he needs in this world, as also the means of rescuing souls from purgatory, and restoring them to the enjoyment of paradise.'

But who, among the princes of Europe, would listen to and finance the dreams of Columbus? Around 1484 a committee appointed by the king of Portugal rejected his plan on scientific grounds. In 1488 Bartholomew, Christopher's brother, crossed to England but could not persuade Henry VII; Charles VIII of France was approached. 'I gave to the subject', Columbus wrote, 'six or seven years of great anxiety.' He went to Spain and undertook his second transformation. For the sake of his idea he was prepared to embrace a new nature, a new nation, a new name; he who was born Cristoforo Colombo, the son of a Genoese weaver, and had become Cristovão Colom of Portugal, now became Cristóbal Colón, gentleman, suitor at the Spanish court. And there, in those forward-looking monarchs Ferdinand and Isabella, he found the rulers with the vision and the means to help him. At first they were repelled by his pretensions and his greed. But finally, when their successful expulsion of the Moors from Spain had shown them their destiny as God's agents, they gave Columbus their commission, in the hope of winning both treasure and souls. On 3rd August 1492, the *Santa Maria*, the *Pinta* and the *Niña* sailed from Palos with ninety men.

On Thursday, 11th October, about ten at night, the sailor Rodrigo de Triana saw a dim gleam like the unsteady light of a wax candle. The Journal of Columbus reported:

Few thought that this was an indication of land, but the Admiral was certain that they were near. Accordingly, they recited the *Salve*, which all sailors are accustomed to sing after their manner, and when they had all gathered together, the Admiral urged them to keep a good lookout from the forecastle and to watch carefully for land, and he promised to give a silk doublet immediately to the first man to cry out land, apart from the other rewards promised by Their Majesties, which were 10,000 maravedis annually to him who first sighted it. Two hours after midnight land appeared, at a distance of about two leagues.

In the morning Columbus dressed in scarlet doublet, took the royal standard of Spain in his hand, went ashore and kissed the ground.

But what ground? Columbus had set out for 'the Indies' and for the realms of the Great Khan, and when he set foot on the tiny island

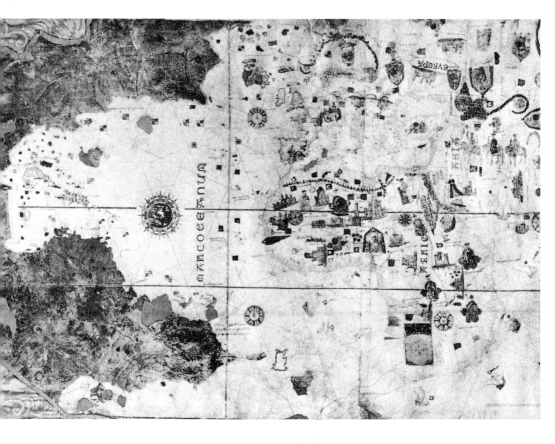

Portolan world map, by Juan de la Cosa, 1500. This portolan, a
sailing chart for mariners rather than a detailed map, is the oldest
representation of the discoveries in the New World. De la Cosa was
the owner and mate of Columbus's *Santa Maria*, and the official
cartographer on Columbus's second expedition. He was killed by
Indians in Venezuela in 1509. The inscriptions on the north part of
the map, 'mar descubierta por yngleses' and 'cavo de ynglaterra',
indicate the discoveries of Cabot in 1497–8.

*Naval Museum, Madrid*

of San Salvador in the Bahamas he was sure that he was at the gate of
the promised land. Marco Polo had spoken of seven thousand islands
in the China Sea; surely San Salvador was one of them; Cipangu would
be nearby, and the great bulk of Cathay not far to the west. At the end
of October, Columbus landed in Cuba, which at first he thought 'must
be the Isle of Cipangu, about which marvellous things are said'; later,
because of the size of the land, he decided that he had reached China:
'It is certain that this is the mainland, and that I am near Zaiton and
Quinsay, about a hundred leagues from either.' He sailed on and

arrived at another large island which he called Española, and this he now took to be Cipangu since here he met gold for the first time.

He left for home convinced that his task was done, that he had opened the western route to the lands of Marco Polo's book. The investment of half a lifetime in an ideal, the pride and obstinacy of discovery, caused him to maintain his self-deception to the end. On his second voyage he made his officers swear that Cuba was the south-east promontory of Asia. On his third voyage he thought that he had found the Earthly Paradise on the coast of South America. On his last voyage he claimed that Central America was Indochina, and that he was only three weeks' journey from the mouth of the Ganges. Was he not, he said, the 'messenger of the new heaven and earth' promised by the Apocalypse?

In April 1493 the court of Ferdinand and Isabella assembled in Barcelona to welcome the return. The Admiral (for so Columbus was now called), granted the honour of remaining seated before his sovereigns, began his tale:

> I, Christo Ferens [Bearer of Christ], have been in the land of the Great Khan from where the spices come. The people are loving and gentle and fit to be Christians. They are docile and will make good slaves. The distance is not half what the mathematicians would have it.

He spoke of the islands he had seen and their naked inhabitants; he spoke of spices and plants and medicinal trees. He demonstrated cages bearing parrots and large tree-climbing rats and small dogs that could not bark. He showed salted fish and skins of large lizards such as had never been seen before; he opened bales of cotton and chests of aloes and spices. He ushered in the poor natives he had brought back and had them sketch the sign of the cross. And at last he uncovered the gold, the masks, the ornaments and the nuggets. It is said that monarchs and court fell on their knees and with tears in their eyes gave thanks to God who had provided such tractable new Christians and such welcome treasures.

It is also related that there was in Valencia about that time another Italian mariner, one Johan Caboto lately of Venice, occupied with plans for docks and harbour-works. In the spring of 1493 Columbus passed through Valencia on his triumphant way to Barcelona. No one knows if Cabot followed him on the dry road north, to hear the tale from the Admiral's mouth. In any case the prizes had been exhibited on the road and the full news was soon the property of Spain. No doubt the story sounded well enough at the first telling: the wonders that Columbus unfolded seemed bright enough against the dusty skies of northern Spain. But John Cabot knew the works of Marco Polo, and Columbus's claim was not convincing. Were these simple savages on show the masterful men of Cathay or Cipangu? Where was the evidence of empire, of administration, of planning, of extensive trade? Where were the cities, the great congregations of people, the products of art and culture? The few crude shapes in gold were pretty, but where were the pearls, the jewels, the silks, the brocades that Polo had seen so abundantly in the east? What evidence was there of architecture, of armies, of pack-animals, of ships? Cabot was a traveller who had been to Mecca and knew something of the geographers and the maps. He saw that Columbus had deceived himself, deliberately under-estimating the vast distance to the east; the lands he had discovered were merely half-way islands. Cabot knew that the way to the Earthly Paradise had yet to be found. He was prepared to risk the venture, and since Spain was committed to Columbus he took his dream and his plans to England.

The earliest known map of Bristol, by Hoefnagle, 1581. The compact city has not yet expanded beyond its late medieval walls.

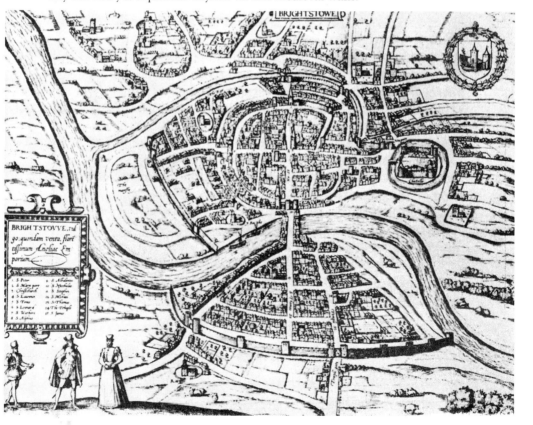

Few sailors knew the northern seas as well as the men of Bristol. West-facing, at the gate of the Atlantic, Bristol had welcomed generations of trade which had made it the second largest city in England. These days of its prosperity saw bales of Cotswold wool going out on the tide while the incoming barrels of Iberian wines were stacked high in the warehouses. West-country fishermen, taking herring and cod where they could, circled the Irish coast, went to Iceland, sailed the open Atlantic waters of the Porcupine Bank, and perhaps beyond. The feet of the Bristol merchant rang familiarly on the docks of the western world, from the Aegean ports to the coves of the Azores.

Silence buries the epic of ordinary voyages. The many years of commerce between Norway and the New World were almost forgotten; the story was barely kept alive by the persistent poets of the sagas until the archeology of a modern age re-assembled the fragments of history. No one knows what chance landfalls were made by merchants or fishermen driven on by curiosity or uncontrollable winds. Las Casas, in his *Historia de las Indias*, recalled an ancient sailor of the Azores who had told Columbus of a journey he once made to Ireland on which he had seen a land far to the west 'that others believed to exist there, and they imagined it was Tartary which projected that way by the east, which I believe truly was that which we now call the Bacallaos [Newfoundland]'. On 15th July 1480 a Bristol ship of eighty tons, under the master John Lloyd, set out to look for the island of Brasil, that mythical island of the mid-Atlantic. Storms and a leaking ship drove them back to Ireland. A year later the *George* and the *Trinity*, also of Bristol, took up the task 'to search and fynde a certain Isle called the Isle of Brasile'. Each ship carried forty bushels of salt, not, as they explained to the customs, for trade but 'for the reparacion and sustentacion of the said shippes'. Salt was needed to bring cod back from far waters in the form of stockfish. Were the two ships fishing on the Newfoundland Banks? Did they put in on the American shore? Were there other exploratory voyages from Bristol? Later sons of the city claimed that there had been such voyages, and successful ones too.

In 1527 Robert Thorne, a Bristol merchant resident in Seville, sent the English ambassador a letter about the possibilities of English exploration. In this letter he mentioned the achievements of his father and other Bristol mariners in the last century: 'So this inclination or desire of discovering I inherited of my father, which with another merchant of Bristol named Hugh Elliot were the discoverers of the

Newfound Lands, of which there is no doubt.' In the winter after Cabot's voyage of 1497, another Englishman in Spain, one John Day, wrote an account of the new discovery for the benefit of a high-ranking Spaniard who was most likely to have been Columbus himself. 'It is considered certain', Day wrote, 'that the Cape of the said land was found and discovered in the past by the men from Bristol who found Brasil, and it is assumed and believed to be the mainland that the men from Bristol found.'

Boasts, lies, misplaced dreams? Or the matter-of-fact claims of men about their normal business? Certainly few had the sea-knowledge and deep-water experience of the Bristol sailors, and a hopeful voyager to the unknown west could not have been in better hands.

John Cabot arrived in Bristol at some uncertain date in the last decade of the fifteenth century. Few of the facts of his life are clear. An Italian, a Renaissance egotist tormented by the thought of so much eastern wealth almost within reach of any bold mariner, he sought the means to possess it with the relentless passion of an idealist. His native land, weakened by the petty jealousies of the independent city-states and coveted by the great powers of France and Spain, could not help his ambition. He went to Spain and Portugal in search of finance, ships and navigators. Neither would assist him, for Spain was committed to Columbus and Portugal had her own plans to round the tip of Africa and cross the Indian Ocean. Why then, he would go to England, for his ambition was intense and personal and, like Columbus, he did not care what flag he sailed under or what nation would claim him in the future.

It was his purpose to redirect the simple, candid efforts of the Bristol sailors. For years, at least since 1480, these men had been making the western passage, fishing on the shallow banks near what they took to be the island of Brasil. If they saw land they saw the harsh granite and dark forests of Newfoundland which no one thought to connect with the airy wonders of Marco Polo's Cathay or Cipangu. Their discoveries were hardly noted, for they raised no hopes of fame or great riches: there was good fishing to be had in the lee of a gloomy land, and that was all. Later generations of Englishmen complained that England had missed her chances in the early days of discovery. 'Yet Henry had a tender of these lands, Which he embrac'd not,' wrote the poet Charles Aleyn recalling the visit of Bartholomew Columbus to the court of Henry VII in 1488–9. If only those pioneer ships of the Bristol merchants had followed the coast of Newfoundland, wrote Robert Thorne in 1527, 'the land of the Indians from whence all the gold commeth had been ours: for all is one coast, as by the card appeareth.' But Henry VII, who was, as the Milanese ambassador noted, 'wise and not lavish', saw neither advantage nor profit in English voyages until the visionary enthusiasm of John Cabot persuaded him that the golden lands stood within reach and that Bristol knew the way there.

Cabot came to Bristol with globes and maps and tempting arguments. He sketched a route to Cipangu, striking down the coast from the land already known to the Bristol captains as Brasil and thus outflanking Spain. His own erroneous geography, so forcefully put, overcame the more simple geographical misconceptions of the Bristol merchants. To these he promised personal riches, to the city corporation he promised undying prosperity from the spice trade which would flow into the port. He contracted with merchants for money, ships and crews. His next task was to gain the royal blessing for his project. In January 1496 the Spanish ambassador, Puebla, was warning his monarchs of 'one like Columbus' intent on 'inducing the King of England to enter upon another undertaking like that of the Indies'.

The North Atlantic, from the Cantino world map, 1502. The line down the middle of the picture acknowledges the division of the New World between Spain and Portugal, according to the Treaty of Tordesillas in 1494. The Portuguese cartographer has claimed all the coasts of Labrador and Newfoundland for Portugal under the title *Terra del Rey de Portugall*, thus ignoring completely the discoveries of Cabot and the English.

*Biblioteca Estense, Modena*

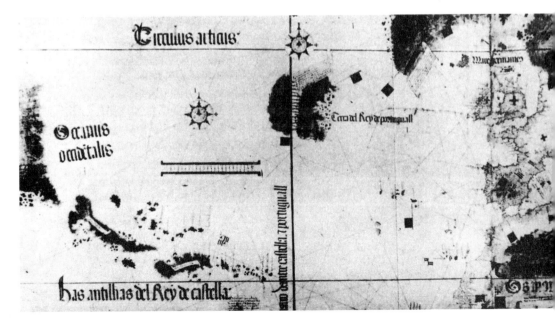

Early in 1496 Henry had received a petition from 'John Cabotto, Citezen of Venice, Lewes, Sebastyan and Soncio, his sonnys' to grant 'your gracious letters patentes under your grete seale in due forme to be made according to the tenour hereafter ensuying'. The king had considered the matter openly with Puebla, for he had no wish to antagonize Spain. He decided that the Cabots might take and hold, as vassals of the English crown, 'whatsoever islands, countries, regions or provinces of heathens and infidels' not already possessed by Spain. He did not believe that Spain had a prescriptive right to all the undiscovered New World; nor did he feel himself bound by the papal Bull and the Treaty of Tordesillas which in 1494 had divided the new discoveries between Spain and Portugal.

So Henry granted letters patent to John Cabot, his sons and their heirs and deputies, to take five ships and find their fortune; to conquer, occupy and possess in the king's name; to trade how and where they would in the new lands so long as all goods were brought back to the port of Bristol where they would be exempt from customs duty. The document was signed on 5th March 1496. Anxious for his rewards, Cabot set out with one ship in the summer of the same year, but was driven back by bad weather and shortage of food. In the next year he was ready to try again.

In the middle of May 1497, the *Matthew*, a small ship of fifty tons, set out from Bristol. Cabot had with him one or two friends, a couple of merchants, the master and the crew—in all no more than twenty people. Of the voyage out there is little record; the master skirted Ireland then turned north before making the great plunge westwards. The sea journey from Dursey Head to Cape Race is not a great distance, and the way was known to the Bristol pilot. But there is no reason to suppose that their loneliness was any the less, or that they were without the familiar, crass fear of the deserted ocean. In fair weather the *Matthew* made the passage in little over a month, coming to land on 24th June—the Feast of St John the Baptist. On the same day Cabot went ashore, named the territory St John in honour of the saint, and took possession by planting a cross and the banners of England, the pope and St Mark of Venice. The day was hot, a track led inland beside a burnt-out fire; the tall evergreens shivered in the slight breeze, and here and there a tree had been notched or felled. The grass was thick. No human or animal cries disturbed the silence, no living creature appeared. The surrounding forest seemed as implacable as a standing army. Cabot drew his men back to the beach where they filled the water-casks at a brook; then 'being in doubt, he returned to his ship'.

For another month Cabot coasted the islands and shores of the New World, but he did not land again. The landfall which he called St John cannot be placed, nor is there any indication of where he went for that month. He noted that the seas were full of fish. At a distance the crew saw vague forms, animal or human, running on the land; they pieced out what appeared to be fields and saw 'a forest whose foliage looked beautiful'. On the return the little *Matthew* made an exceptional passage to Brittany, with fair winds and bright skies all the way. By the end of the first week in August the ship was back in Bristol. On the tenth Cabot was granted an interview with the king.

Cabot brought little enough to show the king, having nothing but a snare, a wooden needle for making nets and some carved sticks as evidence of life. But Henry was pleased. The journey had been first and foremost a flight of the imagination, and merely to land seemed to vindicate the arguments and the vision of Cabot. The public was excited and the commentators in England advanced great claims on this slender evidence and prepared for an extravagant future. Writing to his family from London at the end of August the Venetian merchant Lorenzo Pasqualino announced that Cabot had discovered 'the country of the Great Khan'. A correspondent of the Duke of Milan, writing about the same time, claimed also the discovery of the mythical land of Seven Cities. Soncino, the Milanese ambassador, reported to his master that the king of England 'has gained a part of Asia, without a stroke of the sword'.

The journey of the *Matthew* was only a reconnaissance; now the new lands could be opened up and their excellent treasures revealed. 'They say', wrote Soncino, 'that the land is fine and temperate, and they believe that Brazil wood and silk are native there. They assert that the sea there is swarming with fish, which can be taken not only with the net, but in baskets let down with a stone, so that it sinks in the water.' All along the coast, John Day wrote in the account of the voyage he prepared for Columbus, 'they found many fish like those which in Iceland are dried in the open and sold in England and other countries, and these fish are called in English stockfish'. But fish, valuable though they were, counted for nothing in Cabot's larger dream. 'Messer Zuan [Cabot]', noted the well-informed Soncino, 'has his mind set upon even greater things, because he proposes to keep along the coast from where he touched, more and more towards the east, until he reaches an island which he calls Cipangu, situated in the equinoctial region, where he believes that all the spices of the world have their origin, as well as the jewels.' London would become a more important mart for spices than Alexandria.

Blinded by potential riches England and John Cabot celebrated together. Pasqualino wrote:

> He is called the Great Admiral, and vast honour is paid to him and he goes dressed in silk, and these English run after him like mad, and indeed he can enlist as many of them as he pleases, and a number of our rogues as well.

Henry gave him a pension of £20 and was so far impressed with his deeds as to promise aid for further journeys. He intended to give Cabot ten or twelve armed ships, and also a complement of gaol-birds and malefactors who would be left in the New World to form a colony.

Cabot's headlong purpose, to grab the riches of the east, was reined in and schooled by the practical wisdom of Henry VII. Throughout the autumn and winter of 1497 the king encouraged a debate on the possibilities of the discovery. Ayala, the new Spanish ambassador, complained vigorously that the English plan infringed the rights of Spain. And then Cabot was brought forth with his maps and globes to explain how his route would take him behind the discoveries of Columbus, which were merely some islands in the Atlantic and not the mainland at all. Pressed by the expenses of Perkin Warbeck's rebellion, the king cut down the dozen armed ships of his first offer; eventually only one ship was equipped by the king, and four others by the merchants of Bristol and London. Henry retained the idea of forming a 'colony' of ruffians who would establish a trading-post between England and the far east. Since Henry was a pious Catholic prince, he also sent some friars to convert the heathen. On 3rd February 1498 Cabot received further letters patent to gather his fleet and sail to the 'land and isles of late found by the said John in our name and by our commandment'.

The circumstances of the second voyage are even more mysterious than those of the first. In May the fleet of five ships left Bristol. One ship—it may have been Cabot's—was driven into an Irish port. The rest went on and Cabot followed; afterwards there is no certain news. Polydore Vergil, the king's official historian, writing some years after the event, suggested that Cabot was wrecked and drowned: 'He is believed to have found the new lands nowhere but on the very bottom of the ocean to which he is thought to have descended together with his boat, the victim himself of that self-same ocean; since after that voyage he was never seen again anywhere.'

The end of the visionary mariner marked also the end of his dream. There are hints, no more than tiny indications, that the rest of his fleet survived him and carried out the long westward and southern exploration of the coast which slowly and reluctantly proved to them that here were no cities, no marks of government, no empires, no trade, no silks, no jewels, only the long and savage littoral bordered by unyielding forest speckled with the frightened eyes of timid man and more timid beast. Cathay and Cipangu vanished at a stroke to be replaced by the terse names of 'New Land' or 'New Found Land'. The celebrated riches of Marco Polo disappeared back into the realm

Italian map of the North Atlantic, anonymous and undated, but after 1503. The lands marked were those investigated by the Sailors of Portugal and the Azores—the Corte Reals and the 'labrador' João Fernandes who was later employed by the Bristol adventurers.
*British Museum*

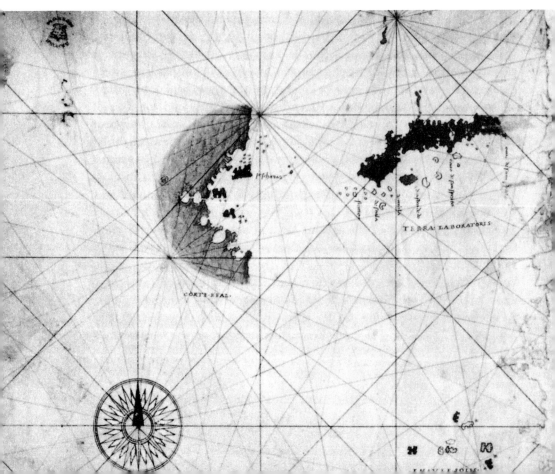

of fables. Instead of a bounteous Asia the explorations of Cabot had uncovered the blank American shore.

A large, unknown land-mass stood between Europe and Asia. Yet some profit might still be salvaged from the wreck of the ancient dream. A way might be found through or around the obstructing land. And that land itself, a virgin area for speculation, had the attraction of unmapped territory. It was forbidding enough at first sight, at least in northern latitudes, but travellers noticed a softer aspect as they went south, the weary rhythm of coniferous forest giving way to the bright and varied hues of broad-leaf woods; exposed granite changed to fields, the sands grew whiter, the sun warmer. And even in the north, the multitudes of fish in the coastal waters and on the shallow ocean banks made the long journey from England worthwhile. The benefit of the fisheries did not escape such a prudent monarch as Henry VII; he also saw, with greater imagination, that an English foothold in the New World gave England a tactical advantage in manoeuvres of European politics. As long as Henry lived the New Found Land was not forgotten, and voyagers had the encouragement of the royal patronage.

The voyages therefore continued, but in a new and quieter spirit. No longer were the expeditions possessed by the inspired enthusiasm of a Columbus or a John Cabot, certain that each day sailed was a progress towards unimaginable wealth. The spices, jewels and metals of Asia were still the ultimate goal, but hard experience had taught caution. The voyages after Cabot were exploratory, seeking ways and means, content to approach the profitable heaven by steps and stages.

At the turn of the century a new possibility arose. The Portuguese, who had always been in the front of discovery, began to probe the waters around Greenland, searching for a northern route to Asia. The leaders of these expeditions, the brothers Corte Real, were lost and the attempt was abandoned; in any case King Manoel had decided to concentrate the Portuguese effort on the Cape route to India which Vasco da Gama had recently opened up. One Portuguese however, a certain João Fernandes from the Azores, believed in the north-west passage, and even while the Corte Reals were on the seas had followed the example of Cabot and brought his plan to the well-practised seamen of Bristol.

On 19th March 1501 Henry VII granted letters patent for an expedition to be led by three men from the Azores and three Bristol merchants: João and Francisco Fernandes and João Gonsalves were described as 'esquires of the Azores'; the Bristol merchants were Richard Warde, Thomas Asshehurst and John Thomas. The grant allowed the same rewards and rights as John Cabot was promised, so long as the grantees avoided all land already in the hands of Christians. But the grant was far longer and more detailed than either of the two given Cabot. The 'arctic and northern seas' are expressly mentioned and trading rights, the handling of merchandise and the payment of fees and dues are covered in exact detail. The grant allowed for the plantation of a colony. It seems that Henry had a statesmanlike plan for the expedition. The captains were to push beyond the land discovered by Cabot, entering the arctic waters between Greenland and the American shore in the hope of finding the north-west passage to Asia. At some point or points the colonists were to be landed—most likely the same desperate ruffians that had been promised to John Cabot—and they would form English settlements to act as trading-posts between Europe and Asia. Stable and wealthy commerce was always the chief end of Henry's policy. Even the most barren land could support a few criminal wretches who would expiate their sins in bitter loneliness, handling goods for the future prosperity of their homeland.

The ships were back by January 1502, for the king's Household Book of that month records a payment of 100 shillings to the 'men of Bristol that found the isle'. Henry was pleased with the expedition which had brought back convincing evidence of enterprise. The London chronicler reported that three men 'taken in the New Found Island' were presented to the king: 'These were clothed in beasts' skins and ate raw flesh and spake such speech that no man could understand them, and in their demeanour like to brute beasts.' Two years later these Eskimos (for such they surely were) still lived in Westminster Palace, but now well-groomed and dressed like English men.

In the summer of 1502 another Bristol expedition had crossed the ocean; on 30th September there was a payment of £20 'to the merchants of Bristol that have been in the New Found Land', and a few days earlier the king had granted pensions of £10 each to Francisco Fernandes and João Gonsalves 'in consideration of the true service they have done unto us, to our singular pleasure, as captains into the New Found Land'. Although the north-west passage was not found, a part of the king's hope seemed to be realized; a small trickle of commerce between England and the New World began.

For a few years the voyages went on hopefully. New patents were issued to various groups of Bristol merchants, who then formed themselves into 'The Company Adventurers of the New Found Lands'.

The Avon Gorge, a prospect familiar to all Bristol sailors. Detail taken from James Millerd's plan of 1673.
*City of Bristol Museum and Art Gallery*

The new territories provided merchandise of a kind. Strange hawks, and parrots, and mountain cats made their appearance in England. The Household Book recorded a payment for 'a brasil bow and two red arrows'. The patents had envisaged colonies, and perhaps some were settled, for in April 1504 'a priest that goeth to the new Island' was paid 40 shillings. What comfort did he manage to bring to the sour lodgings of that first new England, set beside a bay in Labrador, Newfoundland or Nova Scotia, where the rough colonists saw to the needs of the fishing fleet and collected a few commodities—timber, skins, wild animals, simple native artifacts—for the wonder of the citizens in the far-distant homeland? Forty shillings seems a small payment for such an exile.

Detail from the plan of Bristol by James Millerd, 1673. The Rental Books of 1498/9 show that John Cabot had a house in this area, close to the port. The area known as the Marsh, containing the Custom House, was in Cabot's day a boggy piece of open ground outside the city walls.

*City of Bristol Museum and Art Gallery*

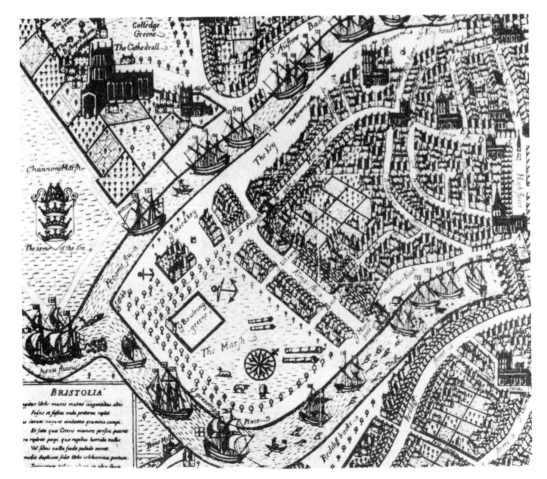

A foot on the alien shore, some trinkets and curiosities, a quantity of fish—but the grand design, the great economic plan to link Europe with Asia, was yet to be achieved. It was time to make another strong effort before the king lost interest in a barren land and the Bristol merchants diverted their ships to less rigorous seas and more profitable ports. And who better to make the attempt than Sebastian Cabot, the son of the old dreamer?

Sebastian was about twenty when his father disappeared in 1498. He had settled in Bristol, and the first decade of the new century saw him prosperous and important in the city; in 1505 the king granted him a pension of £10 as a reward for his services to Bristol. He was, as his later history showed, a merchant, a cartographer and a student of navigation. The letters patent granted to his father were still in force, and the rights under the patent had come down to Sebastian as his father's heir. He was free to make what journeys he liked into the unmapped regions.

The voyage he made in 1508–9 has been the subject of much speculation, for there was no contemporary record of it, and later accounts were muddled versions of an event long past. But the general outline of his journey is not in doubt. He sailed north with two ships and a largish party, heading for the arctic waters. He went beyond the parts where the English had already been and into the waste-lands where the polar bears fished on the seashore. At about 61 degrees north he turned westward and, following the coast for some 10 degrees of longitude, came into a broad sea which spread out to the south and west. This, which was in fact Hudson Bay, he took to be the China Sea and gave thanks that he had found the north-west passage. He could not go on, for some say his crew mutinied and some say he met impassable ice: 'Whence it was necessary for Cabot to turn back without effecting what he intended, but with a resolve to return to that project at a time when the sea should not be frozen. He found the King dead, and his son cared little for such an enterprise.'

The death of Henry VII on 21st April 1509 brought the first age of English exploration to an end. Sebastian Cabot, on his return, was employed as a cartographer without the hope of another expedition. In 1512, with the permission of the English, he transferred to the Spanish service; the Cabots, wherever they might live, were always Italians of the old days before nationalism, putting their individual vision before the service of any nation. For thirty-six years Sebastian lived in Spain, an authority on all matters of discovery and navigation;

Sebastian Cabot portrayed in the later days of his long life when he had become the respected elder statesman of English navigation and discovery.

in 1518 he became Pilot Major of Spain and for four years after 1526 was in South America in command of a Spanish expedition. But he never forgot the north-west passage. In the twenties he was in discussion with Henry VIII and Wolsey about it, and a little later offered the secret to the city of his birth: 'I had the means', he told the Venetian agent, 'of rendering Venice a partner in this navigation, and of showing her a passage whereby she would obtain great profit, which is the truth, for I have discovered it.'

When Henry VIII died and it seemed that England would return once again to the northern seas, Cabot came back to England and pressed the claims of his first voyage; Sir Humphrey Gilbert tells us that Cabot's charts and papers were 'in the Queen's Majesty's privy gallery, at Whitehall' as late as 1566, and in 1583 Richard Hakluyt, the great historian of the voyages, promised the publication of these papers. He never did so, and the papers have now disappeared.

In the last ten years of his life Sebastian Cabot was the respected pioneer of English exploration, the governor of the Muscovy Company, the friend and adviser of all voyagers. Stephen Borough, the navigator of the Russian waters, pictured 'the good old gentleman Master Cabota' coming to Gravesend in the last year of his life to wish an expedition farewell, and so enjoying the festivities that he 'entered into the dance himself amongst the rest of the young and lusty company'. In 1557 Cabot died, being then close to eighty.

Myth and vision, foresight and prudence together wove the modest tapestry of English exploration in the reign of Henry VII. The forceful imagination of the Cabots, which drove men to the known limits of the world in search of Asian riches, was directed and disciplined by the king himself so that whatever was found might be of use to England. On the dangerous journey to the earthly paradise one might profitably step aside to set up trading posts and establish colonies in the new lands. The farsighted experiment of Henry VII was brought to an end by his impetuous son who judged the exploration expensive, the trading unprofitable, and the settlements a waste of manpower: glory was to be won in Europe, not on virgin land across an ugly ocean. But even in his own time Henry VIII was considered unwise and unadventurous. In 1517, John Rastell, the brother-in-law of Thomas More and the author of an *Interlude of the Four Elements*, wrote:

33

O what a thing had been then,
If that they that be Englishmen
Might have been the first of all;
That there should have taken possession,
And made first building and habitation,
A memory perpetual;
And also what an honourable thing
Both to the realm and to the King,
To have had his dominion extending
There into so far a ground,
Which the noble King of late memory,
The most wise Prince, the seventh Harry,
Caused first to be found.

Rastell's ideal awaited other times, other men.

2

# 2

# Preparation

A SMALL COUNTRY, poor and unimportant, under a new Tudor dynasty, could not compete abroad with the great monarchies of Spain and France. The reign of Henry VIII, both by chance and intention, prepared a land for new ventures.

Exploration and far-distant trade could not prosper without sea power. 'He that commands the sea is at great liberty,' wrote Francis Bacon, voicing the experience of the sixteenth century; 'the wealth of both Indies', he continued, 'seems in great part but an accessary of the command of the seas.'

The cautious architect Henry VII gave the start to maritime success. He built few ships, but maintained those that existed, looked after the navy, constructed a dockyard at Portsmouth, and rewarded ship-building by offering bounties to the owners of large vessels. His mercantile policy encouraged sea trade, and his Navigation Acts protected and favoured the English shipowner. In naval matters, as in much else, Henry VIII completed the work of his prudent father. Lover, poet, musician, scholar, sportsman, the young king was a sailor too. He studied the configuration of hulls and knew the relative merits of different riggings and sail plans. He was himself, so the emperor's ambassador wrote, the designer of a certain type of galley. An eye on the wind, a hand on the shrouds, Henry liked to play the royal mariner, dressed in cloth-of-gold and with the pilot's whistle on a golden chain round his neck. It was his policy and his conceit to be the father of the English navy.

He inherited perhaps five ships; at his death he left a navy of some eighty-five vessels of which forty-six were built, twenty-six bought, and thirteen were prizes.

The ships were of varied size and constructed for all types of war-fare; but most, more than in other navies, were designed for the turbulent open seas. The *Henry Grace à Dieu*—the famous *Great Harry*—

About the year 1564 Peter Bruegel made several accurate and closely observed drawings of contemporary ships. Though these are Flemish ships they differed little from English vessels of the same period. The two on the right demonstrate the heavy armament of the man-of-war; while the one on the left, which differs from the fighting ships only in its lack of guns, would seem to be a supply ship or merchantman.

a four-master of 1,000 tons, was the largest of the fleet. Built in 1514, she took 3,739 tons of timber, 56 tons of iron, and cost over £8,000. She was as powerful as any ship afloat, the emblem and the pride of a seafaring people.

Several others, such as the *Great Elizabeth*, the *Gabriel Royal*, the *Sovereign* and the *Matthew*, were almost as large and differed little from the *Great Harry* in armament and equipment. After these dreadnoughts came the mass of the fleet, ranging from 400 tons down to 30 or 40 tons.

The great ships were 'built lofty', with high, cumbersome poops and forecastles to carry the tiers of guns. They were still slow and ungainly, but experiments with sail plans, and especially the introduc-

Small man-of-war, by Peter Bruegel. This print gives a good impression of the very small size of the average warship. The ships that defeated the Armada averaged only some 120 tons each, and even that was large by the standard of the explorers' vessels. The boats on the left are typical oared galleys, with lateen sails, of the Mediterranean pattern. Although occasionally built in England, these boats were never effective in the rough, tidal waters of the English coast.

tion of fore-and-aft sails on the mizzen masts, improved the handling and enabled them to sail closer to the wind. Of the lighter vessels, some had flush decks with gun-ports beneath, some were galleys with both masts and oars, and some were rowed galleys of a Mediterranean pattern. But these last were neither popular nor successful, for the English abhorred galley service and the vessels could hardly be used in English waters 'by reason of the very great strength of the tides'.

A large ship was manned by about 400 soldiers, 260 sailors and 40 gunners. Besides shot and gunpowder, a warship carried armour, pikes, bills, bows and arrows. The boarding of the enemy and the consequent hand-to-hand fighting was still considered an important part of naval strategy.

Man-of-war and galley, by Peter Bruegel. Armament and sail plan are typical of the time. Beside the large guns pointing outward, smaller guns in the forecastle and even in the crow's nest covered the decks and the close approaches to repel boarders. The mainsail has a 'bonnet' attached to its lower edge which was removed in rough weather thus shortening or 'reefing' the sail.

Seventy or eighty guns was the complement of a large ship, and as the reign progressed numerous light pieces were discarded for fewer, heavier guns. Serpentines gave way to curtalls and culverins, some weighing 3,000 lbs and capable of fearful destruction against wooden ships.

A sailor's pay was five shillings a month; officers received the same rate but had extra shares according to rank. In the *Peter Pomegranate*, a typical ship of 450 tons, the master has £1 10s. a month, the mate 10s., the boatswain 12s. 6d., the master gunner, the carpenter, the purser, the steward and the cook 10s. each. The usual food was biscuit, salt beef, herring and beer; the allowance for provisions was 1s. 3d. per man per week. But the supply of food was a constant problem, for the victualling was poorly organized and the merchants were naturally reluctant to sell at the low prices fixed by the royal agents. Captains often complained that their men were made mutinous by poor supplies.

And indeed the seamen were independent and truculent; more than one gentlemanly commander was rough-handled by their 'ungodly manners'. Ferocious regulations could not curb them: a murderer was tied to the corpse and thrown overboard; anyone who raised a hand against the captain had that hand cut off; a thief was ducked two fathoms under and towed behind the ship. But the men would not be disciplined. Slackness and insubordination caused the loss of the *Mary Rose*, the vice-admiral's ship. which capsized in shallow water in July 1545. Her captain, Sir George Carew, admitted that he had on board 'a sort of knaves that he could not rule'.

But when the mood was on them the seamen could fight and sail, which was all that mattered in an age of opportune raids and chance skirmishes. In more than thirty years of careful attention Henry created a large, belligerent navy, well-ordered, experienced and confident. He reformed the administration. His ships were seaworthy, sailed well enough, and could produce the cruellest weight of fire yet seen on the ocean. The sailors were a rough lot but would follow an intrepid commander. Man for man, ship for ship, the English were the best in Europe, and the knowledge of this superiority was enough to give them the command of the sea.

The growth of the navy helped all English maritime enterprise. In time of war the king needed a large merchant fleet to support the navy,

The *Grand Mistress*. This 450-ton ship, built at Smalhithe in 1545, was a fairly typical medium displacement vessel of the Tudor navy. The picture shows that a few large guns had taken over from the numerous lighter pieces of early Tudor ships. Though the *Grand Mistress* fought well against the French in her first action, by 1555 she was finished. In that year she was sold for a derisory £35, an indication of her bad condition.

*British Museum*

either as transports and supply ships or as auxiliary fighting ships; for the bigger merchantman was little different from the man-of-war. So Henry still paid the bounty for the construction of large merchant vessels; in 1544 the owner of the *Mary James*, a Bristol ship of 160 tons, received five shillings a ton expressly 'to courage other our subjects to like making of ships'. The policy worked. In 1531 the Venetian envoy reported that the king of England could arm 150 vessels; twenty years later another Venetian thought that England could command 1,500 sail of all sizes.

The royal passion caused a renewed interest in shipping. Seven hundred ships each year were said to enter Calais harbour (then an English possession). A great port, such as London or Bristol, might have merchantmen of 400 tons, and even the tiny harbours of the

Calais in the first half of the sixteenth century. The town, England's last continental possession, was (until its fall in 1558) the site of the Wool Staple. Since all wool exported to northern Europe had to go through Calais, the harbour saw a great deal of English shipping.

*British Museum*

north Somerset coast could put out vessels of 100 tons or more. The east coast ports sent 149 ships to the Iceland fisheries in 1528, and a further 222, nearly half from the Cinque Ports, fished for herring in the North Sea. And the perilous waters of these northern seas made bold navigators and hardy seamen. The Venetian envoys, representatives of a great trading republic, watched and approved the English ability at sea. Soranzo found 'great plenty of English sailors who are considered excellent for the navigation of the Atlantic'.

Though there were ships and experienced men, much fishing and heavy coastal traffic, distant trade did not expand greatly in the reign of Henry VIII. His father had been a persevering, peaceful prince, good for commerce; Henry VIII had more gaudy ambitions which were not so kind to trade. The first part of the reign was troubled by wars against the Scots and the French so that the king needed to concentrate his maritime resources in home ports. The end of the reign was soured by the religious quarrel; and the Protestant merchants of England had a hard time of it in the Catholic ports of the Mediterranean and the Indies. Moreover, the vigorous trading of the previous reign had raised English commerce to a high level from which it was difficult to advance.

But the English traders were certainly capable of long voyages, even if they had little encouragement to make them. William Hawkins of Plymouth, the father of the famous Sir John, made three long journeys, the last, in 1532, to Guinea and Brazil. Ten years later Chapuys, the emperor's ambassador, implied that English voyages to Brazil were not uncommon.

Nor did exploration and discovery thrive under Henry VIII. Few voyages were made and nothing new was attempted. The London chronicler noted that the king sent one of his naval masters, John Rut, to the north-west in May 1527 with 'two fair ships, well manned and victualled, having in them divers cunning men, to seek strange regions'. One ship was lost; the other, the *Mary Guildford*, went south from Newfoundland and was next seen, to the surprise of the Spaniards, off Puerto Rico in the West Indies. The English sailors told an unlikely tale, how they had met both ice-fields and hot seas in their search for the lands of the Great Khan. Rut managed some trade in the Indies until the enmity of the Spanish drove him home.

In 1536 a London scholar named Master Hore set out in two ships with a party of 'gentlemen of the Inns of Court and of the Chancery, and divers others of good worship, desirous to see the strange things of the world'. This ill-fated amateur frolic reached Cape Breton and travelled north-east along the Newfoundland shore. They saw bears and many penguins, but the natives avoided them. They could not trade and the land provided no food; eventually their own supplies ran out. They took to cannibalism in desperation. At last they captured a French ship, stole its stores and returned home. Hakluyt had the story of this voyage from one of the company, Thomas Butts, who was so changed by pain and horror that his parents could not recognize him.

These journeys, inconclusive or tragic, proved the capability of the British to make long voyages. It only needed a change of opinion, a twist of history, to send them to foreign shores.

In 1527, beating into the astonished Caribbean, the *Mary Guildford* troubled the Spanish calm of the West Indies. An English ship in the preserve of Spain, at the very gate of her riches: the event was sufficiently ominous to be mentioned in the contemporary histories of both Herrera and Oviedo. When the master, John Rut, wished to trade, the Spanish were in some doubt what to do; the inhabitants of Puerto Rico were willing, but those of Santo Domingo drove him off with gunfire. It was a puzzling question whether to trade or fight, for it was certain that the quiet enjoyment of the wealth of the Indies was at an end, and Spain must decide to share her advantages or defend them. Foreigners, French as well as English, had penetrated the select waters. The glimpse of treasures hardly less spectacular than those of the Great Khan guaranteed their return; greed and ambition gave them the will, the sea power forged in Henry's reign supplied the means.

But the religious quarrel soon made trade officially impossible. After Henry divorced his unhappy Spanish queen in 1533 the English, though still able to make private and profitable deals in the Indies, entered the richer parts of the New World at their peril. The hazard was taken up, for the lure of gold was too strong to be ignored. Nationalism, bigotry, occasionally true religious sentiment, added spice to the game. The English crown, still poor and relatively weak, stood aside whilst it winked at the offences of its subjects. Adventurers had in fact the uncontrolled license of riotous free enterprise; it was their pleasure and their profit to harry Spain and her possessions.

The New World became the school of adventure, the test of manhood, the way to wealth and reputation. And those who came at first to steal began in time to covet the land of riches. Confused in motive, spurred on by dreams, the buccaneer was only a short step from the colonist. The New World appeared a desirable empire. Bacon, in his essay *Of the True Greatness of Kingdoms*, saw great things springing from small but thrusting shoots:

> The kingdom of heaven is compared, not to any great kernel or nut, but to a grain of mustard seed; which is one of the least grains, but hath in it a property and spirit hastily to get up and spread. So are there states great in territory, and yet not apt to enlarge or command; and some that have but a small dimension of stem, and yet apt to be the foundations of great monarchies.

Spirit and command came easily to men trained on the lawless sea-roads. John Hawkins, Drake, Raleigh and the other scourges of the Spanish empire in the reign of Elizabeth were the inheritors of a long tradition of piracy. 'The English sailors', ambassador Puebla had written in the time of Henry VII, 'are generally savages.' Hakluyt lamented that the pirates who had delayed the journey of Bartholomew Columbus to England had kept the West Indies out of English hands. All lands countenanced piracy to some extent and in the first part of the sixteenth century the French were as bad as the English. But England, as her sea power increased, raised piracy to an effective policy of state. William Hawkins had given up the troublesome voyages to Brazil for the sake of robbery in home waters, and the king connived at his raids. Hawkins was, says Hakluyt, 'for his wisdom, valour, experience and skill in sea causes, much esteemed and beloved of King Henry.' Robert Reneger of Southampton, another marauder, showed the easiest way to cause the enemy the greatest hurt. In March 1545 he captured a Spanish treasure ship off Cape St Vincent, homeward bound from the Indies, with gold and pearls and sugar, all to the value of 29,315 ducats. He was then (as the Spaniards bitterly complained) seen swaggering at the king's court.

England was grateful to her judicious pirates who kept the enemy in confusion. Four hundred privateers were known in 1563, a venomous swarm that relieved Elizabeth of the need to increase her navy. Petty robbers who tyrannized all shipping in the coastal waters could expect no mercy from her: over a hundred were hanged in the first half of her reign. But she gave letters of marque to any bold adventurer who would tilt at enemies on open waters. She made patriots of pirates (politely called privateers), reprimanding in public the enterprise she encouraged in private. William Hawkins had become mayor of

Plymouth and a Member of Parliament; Robert Reneger had the lucrative post of Comptroller of the Port at Southampton. Knighthoods and the queen's special favour awaited the greater privateers who followed them.

Most men think as their country thinks: the citizen is the unconscious servant of national aspirations. If exploration and oceanic voyages were neglected in the time of Henry VIII it was in large part because the king had other pre-occupations and the country had little interest. Hakluyt, when he set out to write the history of the English voyages, in the middle of Elizabeth's reign, complained of 'the great negligence of the writers of those times, who should have used more care in preserving of the memories of the worthy acts of our nation'. The early voyages were the eccentric outbursts of private initiative, the unofficial flowering of the private imagination. There was no real attempt at colonization because there was so little thought of it.

In hope and ignorance Henry VII had given John Cabot a commission to form a settlement. The hope died early in the face of an

An action of the French fleet off the Sussex coast, July 1545. A large French force under Admiral d'Annebault harassed the south coast in the summer of 1545. Finally the French were driven off without great loss or damage. The picture, which records an attack on Hove and Brighton, shows the suitability of the continental oared galley for landing troops, while the larger sailing vessels have to stand off from the beach.

*British Museum*

inhospitable land, the difficulties of supply and the lack of means. Practical considerations seemed to rule out empire and, after Cabot, there was no talk of possessions or colonies for a long time. Spain made her conquests behind the unyielding swords of men like Pizarro and Cortes. England had sailors but no professional soldiers; she found it hard enough to keep the Scots at bay. The only thought of Henry VIII throughout his long reign was the independence and self-sufficiency of his kingdom. But he made nationalism a religion and taught it to his people so successfully that in time they had the confidence to look outwards and the wish to assert the national power. The English, France warned Denmark at the beginning of Elizabeth's reign, 'were marvellous greedy of dominion and desirous to enlarge the limits of their kingdom'. This warning referred in particular to English designs on Scotland and Ireland; but once launched, who knew where England might be carried by territorial lust?

In the vigour of their confidence the men of Elizabeth looked about them with pride, insolence and curiosity. 'Observe', Thomas Fuller later commented, 'how God set up a generation of military men, both by sea and land, which began and expired with the reign of Queen Elizabeth, like a suit of clothes made for her, and worn out with her.' The paths that had been closed to their fathers were open to them. 'The searching and unsatisfied spirits of the English,' the chronicler John Stow wrote of them, 'to the great glory of our nation, could not be contained within the banks of the Mediterranean or Levant seas, but they passed far towards both the Arctic and Antarctic poles, enlarging their trade into the West and East Indies.'

Old dreams were remembered. Expediency and idealism gave birth once more to numerous projects. Once again it seemed that riches were to be had as never before, new things done as never before. Soon British ships cruised the lonely sea-routes carrying the treasure of the Indies, the furs of Russia, the tragic black cargoes of West African slaves. Speculation buzzed once more. Sebastian Cabot's map, which had been published in Antwerp in 1544, was printed in London in 1549. In 1553 the new age of English discovery began. Willoughby and Chancellor sailed in an attempt to reach China and Japan by the north-east, around the top of Russia. In the same year *A Treatise of the New India*, by Richard Eden, introduced English readers to the great names of exploration, to Columbus, Magellan, Vespucci and many others. Two years later Eden published his *Decades*, a large collection of voyages taken chiefly from the histories and narratives of the continent, but also including an account of the voyages of his old friend Sebastian Cabot. And, as a further spur to the imagination of his countrymen, Eden prefaced his book with a plea for the English colonization of North America. There was a short way to Asia to be found, either by the north-east or the north-west. There were lands to possess, populate and govern.

3

# 3
# Arguments

*A seed is sown:*  At first, a poet's neglected voice borne on casual winds:

> what an honourable thing
> Both to the realm and the king,
> To have had his dominion extending
> There into so far a ground.
> > John Rastell, *The Four Elements* (1517)

VISION mixed with interest. A Bristol merchant, Robert Thorne, long resident in Seville, seeing the triumphs of Spain and anxious to maintain his own country's credit, addressed Henry VIII:

> Most Excellent Prince, experience prooveth that naturally all princes be desirous to extend and enlarge their dominions and kingdoms. Wherefore it is not to be marvelled, to see them every day procure the same, not regarding any cost, peril, and labour, that may thereby chance, but rather it is to be marvelled, if there be any prince content to live quiet with his own dominions. For surely the people would think he lacketh the noble courage and spirit of all other.

And to prevent this bad opinion of the people, the merchant offered to let his sovereign into a secret

> which hitherto, as I suppose, hath been hid: which is, that with a small number of ships there may be discovered divers new lands and kingdoms, in the which without doubt your Grace shall win perpetual glory, and your subjects infinite profit.
> > Robert Thorne, *A Declaration of the Indies* (1513)

*Exhortation:*  Henry VIII, though proud and imperious, did nothing to extend his kingdom. His successors had to be reminded again. Was England to be so negligent and dilatory while the empires of Spain and

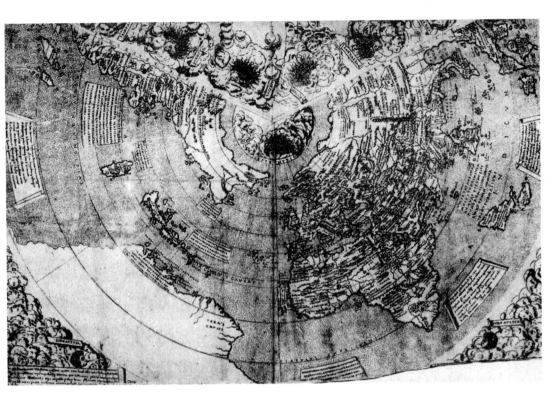

World map by Contarini, 1506. An inscription says: 'The world and all its seas on a flat map . . . Whither away? Stay, traveller, and behold new nations and a new-found world.' This map testifies to the enthusiasm for discovery and contains full, if erroneous, information on the coasts of America, Japan, and the discoveries of the Corte Reals.

*British Museum*

Portugal increased yearly? The success of these countries was the confusion of England:

> Stoop, England, stoop, and learn to know thy lord and master, as horses and other brute beasts are taught to do. Be not indocible like tigers and dragons, and such other monsters noyous to mankind.
> Richard Eden, *The Decades* (1555)

When he considered England's timid part in the history of exploration Eden gave way to rage and contempt, and he filled up his popular accounts of discovery with praise for the effort of Spain and Portugal, and raillery against his native land. His despair was about to end. His own vociferous urgings towards discovery helped to mark the turn of events. Scenting the change of air, old Sebastian Cabot was back from

Spain, a benevolent patron of all navigators. In Mary's reign, Willoughby, Chancellor, Borough and other English captains were testing the various sea routes to the unknown.

*Example:*   The first experience of English colonization in the sixteenth century happened by chance in Ireland, that proving ground of so many grim English jests. Under Mary, in a new attempt to conquer a perpetually hostile land, English settlers were given forfeited estates in Leix and Offaly; and this policy of 'planting' in Ireland, since it cost the crown little, appealed to Elizabeth. The colonies in Ireland, intended to pacify a country, caused rather resistance, brutality and injustice. However, the attempts made a mark in England, particularly with the new breed of speculators and adventurers—the hungry young men of decent birth driven by inflation and lack of places to promote their own ambition at the court. For these were the men employed, as agents of the government, to secure the Irish land and oversee the settlement, while retaining for themselves certain rights and trading monopolies which greatly increased their authority and wealth. It is no surprise that some of the earliest colonizers in the New World, men like Humphrey Gilbert and his half-brother Walter Raleigh, had their first taste of this work in Ireland.

The fields of Ireland festered, the bogs were tinged with blood. Speculators needed safer, quieter places to establish their enterprises. No doubt time would have led them inevitably to the New World. Perhaps their steps were hurried on by examples such as that of Jean Ribault, the French Huguenot sailor who set up a short-lived colony at Port Royal in Florida in 1562 and then came to Protestant England seeking the support that Catholic France would not give him. Ribault's plan was haphazard, his judgement poor and his mistakes serious; in 1565 he was killed in Florida by a Spanish raid. But his venture had seemed to contain good possibilities of success. With better planning and more thought Englishmen might succeed where Ribault had failed.

*The debate:*   Why justify what the heart wants? Reasons make guesses respectable, and daring seem sober; so the reasons for colonization were as numerous and tricky as the men that gave them. Conventional claims, straightforward ambition and secret desires, all jumbled together, conspired to hide true motive. In the clangorous din of lies, self-deception, cunning, curiosity, nobility and faith, the sense of a few recurring themes may be heard.

First, there was nationalism, coverer of many deep sins, and patriotism, nurse of an occasional true love.

The words of Thorne and Eden had been addressed to a sleeping nation. The *Discourse of a New Passage to Cataia*, by Sir Humphrey. Gilbert, written in 1566 but not published for ten years, showed that a man at last was at hand ready to adventure anything to extend the fame and dominion of his country:

> And therefore give me leave without offence, always to live and die in this mind, That he is not worthy to live at all, that for fear, or danger of death, shunneth his country's service, and his own honour, seeing death is inevitable, and the fame of virtue immortal.

No Englishman doubted, in the reign of Elizabeth, that England was now a great land, the equal of France and Spain. She had a right,

North America, by Michael Lok, published in Hakluyt's *Divers Voyages*, 1582. Lok, an experienced traveller, navigator and merchant, drew his map to advertise and support Frobisher's voyages to the north-west. Though based on an 'olde excellent mappe' which Verrazano gave to Henry VIII 'and is yet in the custody of Master Lok', this map clearly shows the new English discoveries and hopefully indicates the wished-for north-west passage.

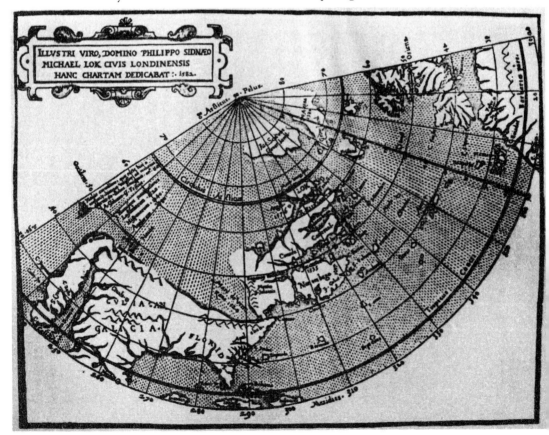

therefore, to take a place in the New World alongside other European nations:

> I marvel not a little (Right Worshipful) that since the first discovery of America (which is now full fourscore-and-ten years), after so great conquest and plantings of the Spaniards and Portugals there, that we of England could never have the grace to set fast footing in such fertile and temperate places as are left as yet unpossessed by them. But, again, when I consider that there is a time for all men, and see the Portugals' time to be out of date, and that the nakedness of the Spaniards and their long hidden secrets are now at length espied, whereby they went about to delude the world, I conceive great hope that the time approacheth and now is that we of England may share and part stakes (if we will ourselves) both with the Spaniard and the Portugal in part of America and other regions as yet undiscovered. And surely, if there were in us that desire to advance the honour of our country which ought to be in every good man, we would not all this while have forslown the possessing of those lands which of equity and right appertain unto us.
>
> Richard Hakluyt, Dedication to Philip Sidney of
> *Divers Voyages touching the Discovery of America* (1582)

It became a commonplace of the adventurers that England had a natural right and lawful title to explore, possess and colonize the lands of North America. Sir George Peckham, with fanciful invention, traced the English title back to the supposed discoveries of the Welsh Prince Madoc in the twelfth century:

> And it is very evident that the planting there shall in time right amply enlarge her Majesty's territories and dominions (or I might rather say) restore her to her Highness ancient right and interest in those countries.
>
> *A True Report of the Late Discoveries* (1583)

Richard Hakluyt, the apostle of English expansion, also accepted the wishful descent from Madoc. 'The Queen of England's title,' he wrote in his *Discourse of Western Planting*, 'to all the West Indies, or at least to as much as is from Florida to the arctic circle, is more lawful and right than the Spaniards, or any other Christian Princes.' Other Englishmen, cruder fellows than the scrupulous deluded Hakluyt, asserted the English title without caring how it came about. The essential thing, as Sir William Pelham expressed it, was to cut out Spain and Portugal, for God and justice were naturally with the English:

Then England thrust among them for a share,
Since title just, and right is wholely thine:
And as I trust the sequel shall declare,
Our luck no worse than theirs before hath been.
For where the attempt on virtue doth depend:
No doubt but God will bless it in the end.
*Commendatory Verses to Sir George Peckham* (1583)

A feeling of loss, of time passing empty-handed, magnified a Welsh chieftain into an ancestral prince of the Indies. A remnant, perhaps a delusion, of Christian duty made conquest a godly and necessary work. The best men, such as the minister Richard Hakluyt, preached charity and the gentle conversion of the Indians. He lamented that England would never prosper abroad until his countrymen observed some of Christ's principles:

I trust that now, being taught by their manifold losses, our men will take a more godly course and use some part of their goods to His glory; if not, He will turn even their covetousness to serve Him, as He hath done the pride and avarice of the Spaniards and Portugals.
Dedication, *Divers Voyages* (1582)

For Hakluyt, the extension of Christendom was the first purpose of colonization, as he declared at the head of the first chapter of his *Discourse on Western Planting*:

That this western discovery will be greatly for the enlargement of the gospel of Christ.

And he thought that the rulers of England had a particular religious duty because 'the Kings and Queens of England have the name of Defenders of the Faith', Elizabeth being in English eyes the principal monarch of the Reformed faith. The enlargement of Christ's kingdom ought to be, not her last work, 'but rather the principal and chief of all others, according to the commandment of our Saviour'.

Hakluyt's declaration was merely the wistful expression of an idealist and churchman. Elizabeth knew nothing of this exalted purpose, and her subjects on the seas had at best an unsure grasp of Christian principle. It was conventional to give religion as a cause for colonization. Spain and Portugal had conquered in the name of Christ, and if England was to enter on a similar course of rapine and extortion it was fitting to do so in the best possible cause. Sir George Peckham, in 1583,

58

wrote of colonization as 'a thing likewise tending to the honour and glory of Almighty God' and insisted that 'the use of trade and traffic (be it never so profitable) ought not to be preferred before the planting of Christian faith'. And Christopher Carlile, in his *Discourse* also of 1583, spoke of 'reducing the savage people to Christianity and civility'. These statements were hardly evidence of a fervent desire to evangelize. Among the English seamen of the sixteenth century only John Davis believed truly in the evangelical mission of Protestant England:

> There is no doubt that we of England are this saved people, by the eternal and infallible presence of the Lord predestined to be sent unto these Gentiles in the sea, to those Isles and famous Kingdoms, there to preach the peace of the Lord: for are not we only set upon Mount Zion to give light to all the rest of the world? Have not we the true handmaid of the Lord to rule us unto whom the eternal majesty of God hath revealed his truth and supreme power of Excellency? By whom then shall the truth be preached, but by them unto whom the truth shall be revealed? It is only we, therefore, that must be these shining messengers of the Lord, and none but we.
>
> *The Worldes Hydrographical Description* (1595)

For the rest, the spreading of the gospel was only a pious hope to sweeten a more wordly and selfish ambition. The *Discourse* (written in 1566) of Sir Humphrey Gilbert, the first Elizabethan document of colonization, does not mention the conversion of the natives. Eighteen years later Hakluyt reluctantly agreed that English exploration was no triumph for Christianity. In his *Discourse on Western Planting* he wrote:

> The Papists confirm themselves, and draw others to their side, showing that they are the true Catholic Church because they have been the only converters of many millions of infidels to Christianity. Yea, I myself have been demanded of them, how many infidels have been by us converted.

And the English clergyman sadly admitted that he could not name one. Far from being witnesses for faith, the English, Hakluyt complained, would rather perjure themselves for the sake of trade, conniving at Romanish practices and cynically appearing as Catholics in Spanish ports: 'The covetous merchant wilfully sendeth headlong to hell from day to day the poor subjects of this realm.'

59

Title-page to the influential *Discourse on Western Planting* written by
Richard Hakluyt in 1584.

By the light of their times these English adventurers were not god-
less, though they were grasping and brutal. A belief in divine providence
bore them up among the manifest dangers of their appalling days, and
they gave thanks to a stern God. The instructions which old Sebastian
Cabot issued in 1553, as Governor of the Company 'for the discovery
of regions, dominions, islands and places unknown', forbade blasphemy,
swearing, gambling and brawling, ordered morning and evening
prayer to be held daily on board ship, and 'the Bible or paraphrases to
be read devoutly and Christianly to God's honour, and for His grace
to be obtained and had by humble and hearty prayer of the navigants
accordingly'. Drake, on his circumnavigation, ordered the whole
company of the *Golden Hind* to take Holy Communion; he was so
displeased by the unchristian conduct of his chaplain that he publicly
excommunicated him and made him wear the legend 'Francis Fletcher,
the falsest knave that liveth'. But their religion included no respect for
the rights of others and little charity for poor heathens. God had
provided them with new lands to be plundered and would succour
them while they did so. Expecting death daily, they faced the end
resolutely, seizing their chances in the great predatory game, and
when they fell, going down in glory.

There also appeared among the arguments for colonization an
obscure sense of social purpose. Tudor England was in trouble.
Ungovernable inflation terrorized aristocrat, landed gentry and
smallholder alike. The countryside was sown with misery as the changes
in agriculture, specially the enclosures of the sheepfarmers, deprived
the rural worker of a livelihood. The unruly towns were swollen with
fugitives and unemployed. Masterless men menaced the roads,
criminals prospered, vagabondage was increasing, the gallows were
busy. Any plan to ease the social unrest at home might seem attractive.

For the second expedition of John Cabot, in 1498, Henry VII had
promised certain malefactors to form a trading post in the new-found
territory. At the beginning of Elizabeth's reign, with the gaols over-
burdened and the dark web of lawlessness constricting the land, the
scheme to export criminals as colonists was once more appealing. In
1566, Gilbert's *Discourse* tentatively restated the benefits:

> Also we might inhabit some part of those countries, and settle
> there such needy people of our country, which now trouble the
> commonwealth, and through want here at home, are inforced to
> commit outrageous offences, whereby they are daily consumed with
> the gallows.

But the expulsion of criminals was a desperate expedient which did nothing to cure the ills at home. Gilbert also had more persuasive arguments aimed at increasing employment at home and strengthening English industry. The needs of exploration and the maintenance of colonies 'shall increase both our ships, and mariners, without burdening of the state'. Providing for the trade with the natives would 'set poor men's children to learn handicrafts, and thereby to make trifles and such like, which the Indians and those people do much esteem: by reason whereof, there should be none occasion to have our country cumbered with loiterers, vagabonds, and such like idle persons'. And best reason of all, the new lands would provide a new market for the all-important English cloth trade:

> They would have the clothes of this our country, so that there would be found a far better vent for them, by this means, than yet this realm ever had.

These were forceful reasons and the propagandists of planting were eager to stress them. Sir George Peckham, who was connected with Gilbert's last expedition and whose *True Report* of 1583 is in large part an echo of Gilbert, spoke of the curing of idleness, the benefits to English shipping and fishing, and the increase of the cloth trade:

> It is well known that all savages, as well those that dwell in the South, as those that dwell in the North, as soon as they shall begin but a little to taste of civility, will take marvellous delight in any garment, be it never so simple; as a shirt, a blue, yellow, red, or green cotton cassock, a cap, or such like, and will take incredible pains for such a trifle.

Hakluyt saw these advantages. His *Discourse on Western Planting* recommended colonies as a means 'to supply the wants of all our decayed trades', and 'for the manifold employment of numbers of idle men, and for breeding of many sufficient, and for utterance of the great quantity of the commodities of our realm'. He also thought, with a kindly prejudice, that English settlers would be more just and temperate towards the Indians than the Spaniards or the Portuguese.

Whatever the plausible reasons, whatever high ideals were given, the chief aim of the sixteenth-century colonizers was riches. Haunted by memories of Marco Polo, desolated by the success of Spain, the pages of the writers ache with longing for treasure. In 1513, Robert

Thorne had tried to tempt Henry VIII with talk of an easy voyage to 'the richest lands and islands of the world of gold, precious stones, balms, spices, and other things that we here esteem most'. 'I see that the preciousness of these things', he later told the English ambassador in Spain, 'is measured after the distance that is between us, and the things that we have appetite unto.' The more that appeared of this wealth, and the more it fell into the hands of others, the more ravening became the English appetite. Gilbert pressed for 'a new passage to Cataia' because:

First, it were the only way for our princes to possess the wealth of all the east parts of the world, which is infinite.

Expanding on the advantage of the passage, he added:

Also we may sail to divers marvellous rich countries . . . trades and traffics, where there is to be found great abundance of gold, silver, precious stones, cloth of gold, silks, all manner of spices, grocery wares, and other kinds of merchandise of an inestimable price.

*Discourse of a New Passage to Cataia* (1566)

Colonization would put England in touch with all these. Nor was that all: virgin lands and temperate climates would give the colonists the pick of the world's commodities, mineral, vegetable, animal. The pages of the propagandists rustle with the susurrus of good things, an incantation to the bountiful life. Listen to Thorne in 1527:

There is no doubt but that the islands are fertile of cloves, nutmeg, mace, and cinnamon: and that the said islands, with other there about, abound with gold, rubies, diamonds, balasses, granates, jacincts, and other stones and pearls, as all other lands, that are under and near the equinoctial. For we see, where nature giveth anything, she is no nigard. For as with us and other, that are aparted from the said equinoctial, our metals be lead, tin, and iron, so theirs be gold, silver, and copper. And as our fruits and grains be apples, nuts, and corn, so theirs be dates, nutmegs, pepper, cloves, and other spices. And as we have jet, amber, crystal, jasper, and other like stones, so have they rubies, diamonds, balasses, saphires, jacincts and other like.

*Letter to the English Ambassador*

Peckham and Hakluyt, bringing together the evidence of the travellers, promised the woods full of game and furs, the air dark with birds, the fields fruitful, the waters heavy with fish; rare trees, rare plants, rare fruits, rare animals; harvests twice a year; rosin, pitch, tar, turpentine, frankincense, wax, rhubarb, cochineal, olive and castor oil: 'A good climate, healthful, and of good temperature, marvellous pleasant, the people good and of a gentle and amiable nature, which willingly will obey, yea be contented to serve those that shall with gentleness and humanity go about to allure them.' Englishmen, the new land made you welcome, inevitable riches waited.

*The promised land:* Though unsure of England's purpose, all agreed on her place in the New World. Sense and history pointed to the northern part of America. Spain and Portugal were firmly set in central and south America. Of the four parts of the world, Robert Thorne told Henry VIII in 1513, three were already in the hands of other princes:

> So that now rest to be discovered the said north parts, the which it seemeth to me, is only your charge and duty. Because the situation of this your realm is thereunto nearest and aptest of all other.

Spain, France and England all coveted the north, but none had the right of possession. From Florida to Newfoundland, Richard Eden wrote in his preface to *The Decades* (1555), were lands 'not yet known but only by the sea-coasts, neither inhabited by Christian men'. Eden urged his countrymen to settle these lands. The Cabots had made the discovery of the northern shores in the service of Henry VII; by right of this discovery Hakluyt claimed for England all lands 'from Florida northwards to 67 degrees (and not yet in any Christian prince's actual possession)'.

The early history of English colonization was therefore a part of England's attempt to enter into her northern inheritance. The Cabots had found the north so barren that for half a century none but fishermen bothered with it. But it was all that was left for England, and in the great reawakening of discovery after 1553 the enthusiasts were hard at work finding the virtues of the north. Robert Thorne, that man of foresight, in 1527 gave the prophetic motto for faint English hearts, urging them north with the bold words: 'There is no land unhabitable, nor sea innavigable.' In 1566 Sir Humphrey Gilbert began the long English search for the north-west passage. His first aim was to drive through by a new, short route to the riches of the east. And this exploration would have the secondary benefit of revealing to the English the

64

still hidden resources of north America. The disciples of Gilbert, who seized on the idea of settlement in those territories, wrote to persuade their readers that, far from being a lonely wilderness, north America was a beguiling land with something for all tastes. Hakluyt recommended America as a chest filled with delightful variety, 'being answerable in climate to Barbary, Egypt, Syria, Persia, Turkey, Greece, all the islands of the Levant sea, Italy, Spain, Portugal, France, Flanders, High Alemania [Germany], Denmark, Eastland, Poland, and Muscovy'. Peckham, addressing his *True Report* to future colonists, was equally reassuring:

And first to bend my speech to the noblemen and gentlemen, who do chiefly seek a temperate climate, wholesome air, fertile soil, and a strong place by nature whereupon they may fortify, and there either plant themselves, or such other persons as they shall think good to send to be lords of that place and country: to them I say, that all these things are very easy to be found within the degrees of 30 and 60 aforesaid, either by south or north, both in the continent, and in islands thereunto adjoining at their choice: . . . so that they may seat and settle themselves in such climate as shall best agree with their own nature, disposition, and good liking: and in the whole tract of that land, by the description of as many as have been there, great plenty of mineral matter of all sorts, and in very many places, both stones of price, pearl and crystal, and great store of beasts, birds, and fowls both for pleasure and necessary use of man are to be found.

Persuasive words needed attempts to prove them.

4

# 4

# The Attempt of
# Captain Thomas Stukeley

*He preferred rather to be sovereign of a molehill than the highest subject of the greatest king in Christendom.*

FURIOUS in action, as intrepid at the moment of death as in all his life, Thomas Stukeley died on the forlorn field of Alcazar, where three kings fell, on 4th August 1578. An unknown grave in Morocco abruptly terminated the wayward and circuitous wanderings of his gaudy span of fifty-odd years: time and temperament had taken him far from Devon, the pastoral land of his beginnings. His family was among those members of the gentry who had prospered with the Tudors, acquisitive landowners, collectors of confiscated monastic property, dabblers in business not beyond petty usury, interested, like so many in the country, in the sea and maritime affairs. Some said he was the bastard son of Henry VIII, and the tale was believed because his life showed a pride and insolence that were more than royal. The sixth of eight children, he felt the pinch of the younger son without land, title or place, whose small income disappeared in the consuming maw of inflation. The best hope for these young men was to rise in the retinue of a great lord, and eventually to find a place at court; doubtless with this in view Stukeley entered the service of the Duke of Suffolk. He learnt the arts of love and war, acquired some scholarship and more boldness. Like so many confident adventurers he had an easy way with languages; a later flatterer commended him, with good reason, on his 'perfect under-standing and almost natural speaking' of foreign tongues. Hot-headed and ambitious, he lived expensively and carelessly. 'Having prodigally misspent his patrimony,' wrote one of his numerous critics, 'he entered on several projects (the issue general of all decayed estates).'

Both his talents and failings marked him out for war. His patron,

Although no authentic portrait of Stukeley has survived, this drawing is alleged to be of him. It certainly portrays the type of debonair gallant to which Stukeley belonged, expensively dressed, formidably armed.

the Duke of Suffolk, died in 1545. Perhaps a year before Stukeley had seen his first action at Boulogne in France; soon after he was a young captain in the garrison at Berwick Castle facing the Scots. For the rest of his disordered life his presence anywhere indicated war or the likelihood of war. He became an agent of chaos, eagerly promoting by force, intrigue or deceit the confusion and lawlessness which allowed him to bend the moment to his advantage. An obscure involvement in a conspiracy against Northumberland in 1550 revealed to him early the possibilities of treachery. In his reckless self-seeking he was impartially disloyal, a lover of stratagems and subterfuges. His brazen deception made his information incalculable. 'We here be amazed how to interpret the tales and judge of the man,' wrote the Council after Stukeley had betrayed the plans of his protector, the French king, to the English government. Naturally, he saw the inside of prison, for he was dangerous to all settled authority. But in an imperfect and machiavellian world of polity he had his uses, and he avoided the penalties worthy of his sins.

The contradictory qualities of bravery, insolence and dishonesty fascinated the despotic monarchs of the age. Though they had an affection for his bravado, on the whole they felt better when he was out of the realm and so they recommended him to one another in the warmest terms. Stukeley marched through Europe in the part of mercenary captain, hoping for the spoils of war to fill his always insatiable purse. He fought for the French king against the Spanish emperor, and for the Spanish emperor against the French king. He campaigned in Picardy and Artois, witnessed the wearisome attrition in the Low Countries where the Emperor Charles battled to keep hold of the Spanish Netherlands. Stukeley found neither the plunder nor the opportunities that he had expected. He had in the past, he boldly wrote to Queen Mary, 'consumed that for which I am in credit' for the service of England, and begged for permission to return to his native land to restore his fortune. In October 1554 he petitioned the queen from the imperial camp at Hesdin:

Because I must look forward to ceasing my service here (where I am before an enemy, of whom if I be taken, I despair utterly of grace or liberty), and to returning to my native country, where I intend to lead my life, I am constrained to have recourse unto you, beseeching you to relent my miserable condition, to tender mine earnest request, to take order that I may attend on the Duke [of Savoy] in England, exempted from all danger and arrest by reason of my debts.

Permitted to return to England, Stukeley took the elementary step by which so many adventurers try to shore up tottering fortunes. He looked for a city heiress and found Anne Curtis, the grand-daughter of an alderman, who agreed to marry him by candlelight against the good advice of her family. Whether from spectacular intemperance or from the prudent intervention of the Curtis family, his marriage failed to cure his habitual feckless life. Soon after the wedding a warrant was issued in Devonshire for Stukeley's arrest on the serious charge of counterfeiting. The affair is yet another puzzle in the incomplete annals of his shadowy existence. It is certain that he escaped, fleeing by sea; and to the sea he now turned his attention, remembering the maritime traditions of his Devon ancestors.

The year 1557 found him living in some style at Aldgate, in London, the owner of a ship called *Anne*, which he bought for £220, and whose journeys he directed from the ease of his 'naked bed'. In another year he had four ships which were available for any sea enterprise. And since privateering was the best business for a bold adventurer with an armed ship, Stukeley transferred his martial talent from land to sea, persuaded that the plundering of enemy merchant ships was both patriotic and profitable work. But unhampered as he was by any sense of morality or law, and not caring to make distinctions, he soon drifted from privateering to plain piracy. In 1558 the report of his indiscriminate attacks off the coasts of Devon and Cornwall reached the Council who bound him over, for the large sum of £500, to answer the case before the Lord Admiral. As so often, luck or connections aided him; Strangwish, his piratical colleague, was gaoled but Stukeley went free; the Admiral decided that he could not 'find matter sufficient to charge Stukeley withal', the result perhaps of a plea to the queen on his behalf made by a high-ranking Spaniard.

Stukeley had a way with great men, and a lucky choice of patrons always served him well. On the death of Queen Mary, towards the end of 1558, the Spanish influence in England went sharply into decline, but by then Stukeley was safely under the wing of Lord Robert Dudley, a favourite of the new Queen Elizabeth, and soon, as the Earl of Leicester, to be one of the great men of the kingdom. The first years of the new reign were cheerful times for Thomas Stukeley. He was known at court, a minor but particularly fiery star in the constellation of Robert Dudley; his manly swaggering presence brought him to the notice of the queen, and the very defects of character were likely to please her cool and cynical mind. 'Lusty Stukeley' he was known as, a splendid and dangerous animal.

In November 1559 old Sir Thomas Curtis, his wife's rich grand-father, died. And at once Stukeley was at hand to squander the laborious accumulations of a long business career on a pleasant course of riotous conduct. What acumen and hardwork and infinite cunning had so carefully built up, Stukeley demolished in two short years of drink, gambling and ostentation, a truly profligate career that was the delight of the ballad-maker:

72

He was no sooner tomb'd––but Stukeley he presum'd
  To spend a hundred pound a day in waste.
The greatest gallants in the land––had Stukeley's purse at their
    command
  Thus merrily the time away he past

Taverns and ordinaries––were his chiefest braveries
  Golden angels there flew up and down.
Riots were his best delight––with stately feasting day and night
  In court and city thus he won renown.

By the end of 1562 the inheritance was gone and the bills were piled
high. 'Borrowing everywhere, paying nowhere', as a critic reported,
he returned to where he started, no more than a debt-ridden captain
in the Berwick garrison. But in the desperate and splendid years of
his manhood he had made a mark on his times. The lawless acts of
pillage, the violent search for money by any means, contrasted para-
doxically with the gallant extravagance, the noble bearing, the
physical bravery and the open-hearted generosity. There was nothing
mean-minded or small about him; no imaginative possibility seemed
beyond him and all who went with him felt the benefit of his large
spirit. Soldiers spoke of his 'royalty to men at arms'. His money and
affection (if not his loyalty) were given without stint: 'what friend', it
was said, 'remains unrecompensed of any friendship towards you?'
Monarchs, dukes, gentlemen, common soldiers, also ale-house keepers
and serving-wenches, acknowledged his peculiar charm. The great
Irish leader Shane O'Neill, who was at Elizabeth's court for the six
months before May 1562, thought Stukeley the most attractive man
in England. 'Many of the nobles, magnates, and gentlemen of that
kingdom', O'Neill wrote, 'treated me kindly and ingenuously, and
namely one of the gentlemen of your realm, Master Thomas Stukeley,
entertained me with his whole heart, and with all the favour he could.'
But what now for Stukeley? In 1562 the money was at an end, the
fires of conspicuous revelry washed out by familiar poverty.

He had his ships still––the *Anne Stukeley* and the *Fortune Stukeley*; he
had the experience of the sea gained in his piratical years; best of all,
he still had the goodwill of the court and the support of Lord Robert
Dudley. Having cast away his fortune Stukeley now 'entered on several
projects' (Thomas Fuller wrote) 'and first pitched on the peopling of
Florida, newly found out in the West Indies'. Jean Ribault, the French
navigator, brought the tale of Florida to England; no doubt Dudley,
a champion of English exploration and seamanship, saw Stukeley as

the man to seize the opportunity so suddenly presented.

It may be said that all European interest and expansion in the New World was a jealous imitation of Spain and Portugal. France was the first to challenge their dominion, and their casual division of the new discoveries between them. War between France and Spain—the contending giants of Europe—had been going on intermittently since the early part of the sixteenth century. Long before the age of Drake and Raleigh the French corsairs had learnt the weakness of the Spanish empire, attacking the isolated Spanish settlements in the Caribbean and Central America in swift forays, relying on adroit seamanship and superior fire-power to stalk, harry and break up the cumbersome treasure fleets from the Indies.

In the twenties Jean Ango, Jean Fleury and other members of a piratical school descended on the Spanish Main from Dieppe and the Breton ports. Later, the sea affairs of France were complicated by the religious quarrel between Catholics and Protestants. The Admiral of France, Gaspard de Coligny, was a Protestant Huguenot, and most of the navigators, who relied on his energetic patronage, were also Huguenots. Coligny imagined an alliance of Protestant sea power—Huguenot, Dutch and English—directed against Spain. He also encouraged colonization, seeing it as a way to relieve Huguenots from the misery of persecution. In 1555 Villegagnon established Fort Coligny on the present site of Rio de Janeiro in Brazil. The settlement endured for four years, weakened by religious differences which were an ironic and faithful copy of the quarrel back home in France. In 1559 the Portuguese captured the fort and brought the experiment to an end. Three years later, in February 1562, the Huguenot Jean Ribault sailed for Florida leaving behind a land about to fall into the Wars of Religion.

In two months he had sailed to a quieter shore, low and gentle, 'the country seeming unto us plain, without any show of hills', but covered 'with an infinite number of high and fair trees'. The water was shallow, with many bars, and navigation difficult against a long and featureless coastline. On 1st May he landed at the mouth of a river and set foot on a land as mild and agreeable as any he had hoped for. With caution and growing confidence he spent the next six weeks exploring the new territory, up and down the many rivers which he named after the fair streams of France—the Seine, the Somme, the Loire, the Garonne, the Belle à Voir. On the third day, in gratitude and hope, Ribault had marked their arrival with a stone pillar carved

74

with the royal arms of France; going ashore to set it up 'we espied on the south side of the river a place very fit for that purpose upon a little hill compassed with cypress, bays, palms and other trees, and sweet pleasant smelling shrubs, in the middle whereof we planted the first bound or limit of his majesty'. Three weeks later they marked another boundary of the French king's new dominion with a column by 'a fair lake of fresh water very good' and 'one of the fairest and best fountains that a maid may drink of'.

All that they had met—the land, the water, the animals, the Indians, the climate—invited a settlement. They decided that no place was better than the river and the sound which they had named Port Royal, and which still bears that name. And there by a creek they built a protective stockade which was called Charlesfort, and chose among themselves the first colonists: 'Many of them offered to tarry there, yea with such a good will and jolly courage, that such a number did thus offer themselves as we had much ado to stay their importunity. . . . How be it, we have left there but to the number of 30 in all, of gentlemen, soldiers, and mariners.'

By the beginning of June Ribault was ready to leave, satisfied that his small settlement was well planted and in safe hands. He warned those that stayed to give 'good and loving behaviour of themselves towards this poor and simple Indians' and sailed from Port Royal on the ninth, taking with him the gifts of friendship and portents of a hopeful future, 'the fan of hernshaw [heron] feathers dyed in red, and a basket made of palm-boughs after the Indian fashion, and wrought very artificially, and a great skin painted and drawn throughout with the pictures of divers wild beasts so lively drawn and portrayed, that nothing lacked but life'.

When Ribault returned to France, on 20th July 1562, he found his native land in the midst of the religious war. He fought on the Protestant side until the peace of March 1563; then, despairing of finding any help for his infant colony in France, he crossed to England. The full story of his venture was eagerly awaited beyond the Channel, for the English claimed a title to all the east coast of North America by virtue of the Cabots' discoveries. Within two months of landing Ribault published, in English, *The Whole and True Discovery of Terra Florida*, a work with many signs of haste and carelessness, but confirming the happiest expectations of Englishmen. It is said that Queen Elizabeth offered Ribault a house and a salary of 300 ducats.

The simple faith of Ribault (and of René de Laudonnière whose

75

*Description of Florida* Hakluyt later translated) was that the French had stumbled into paradise. From the first moment when, closing into the Florida shore, Ribault had been struck 'with an inspeakable pleasure of the odiferous smell and beauty of the same', the French had found nothing but good.

> We entered and viewed the country thereabout, which is the fairest, fruitfullest and pleasantest of all the world, abounding in honey, venison, wildfowl, forests, woods of all sorts, palm trees, cypress, cedars, bays, the highest, greatest and fairest vines in all the world with grapes accordingly, which naturally and without man's help and trimming grow to the top of oaks and other trees that be of a wonderful greatness and height. And the sight of the fair meadows is a pleasure not able to be expressed with tongue, full of herons, curlews, bitterns, mallards, egrets, woodcocks, and of all other kind of small birds, with harts, hinds, bucks, wild swine, and sundry other wild beasts as we perceived well both then by their footing there and also afterwards in other places by their cry and braying which we heard in the night time. Also there be cunnies [rabbits], hares, guinea cocks in marvellous number, a great deal fairer and better than be ours, silk worms, and to be short it is a thing inspeakable, the commodities that be seen there and shall be found more and more in this incomparable land, never as yet broken with plough irons, bringing forth all things according to his first nature, whereof the eternal God endued it.

The land was well watered, 'full of havens, rivers and islands', and the climate was so good 'that none of all our men, though we were there in the hottest time of the year, the sun entering into Cancer, were troubled with any sickness'. This beneficent climate was reflected in the good health of the natives: 'The people there live long and in great health and strength, so that aged men go without staves, and are able to do and run like the youngest of them, who only are known to be old by the wrinkles in their face and decay of sight.'

In the rich soil all manner of growing things sprang up in profusion. Besides the trees that Ribault mentioned, de Laudonnière noted oaks, mulberry, black cherry, holly, chestnut. There were plum trees and medlars, 'the fruit whereof is better than that of France, and bigger'; raspberries and blueberries grew, and peppers waiting to be picked untended by man. The Indians cultivated maize, which was new to the French, and planted beans, gourds, cucumbers, lemons, peas, 'and many other simples and roots unknown to us'. The seas by the sandy shores and the wide waters of the shallow rivers gave up fish without effort, 'that ye may take them without net or angle, as many as you will'; lobster, crayfish, oysters and all kinds of shellfish added variety to the harvest from the water. The land was equally prodigal, supporting familiar domestic animals and animals of the hunt, but with many wild or exotic beasts not often met in Europe, such as wolves, wild dogs, leopards, ounces [lynxes], 'and a certain kind of beast that differeth little from the lion of Africa'; there were also more dreadful creatures like crocodiles and many serpents.

And most happily, all this goodness, all this generosity of nature was presided over by a gentle, friendly people. The first meeting, as Ribault's landing boat edged cautiously to shore, was marked by simple native dignity and openness:

We perceived a good number of the Indians, inhabitants there, coming along the sands and seabank somewhat near unto us, without any token of fear or doubt, showing unto us the easiest landing place, and thereupon we giving them also on our part tokens of assurance and friendliness, forthwith one of the best of appearance among them, brother unto one of their kings or governors, commanded one of the Indians to enter into the water, and to approach our boats, to show us the easiest landing place. We seeing this, without any more doubting or difficulty, landed, and the messenger, after we had rewarded him with some looking glasses and other pretty things of small value, ran incontinently towards his lord, who forthwith sent me his girdle in token of assurance and friendship, which girdle was made of red leather, as well cured and coloured as is possible. And as I began to go towards him, he set forth and came and received me gently and reysed [saluted] after their manner, all his men following him with great silence and modesty, yea, with more than our men did.

The good impression of the first meeting was confirmed in the six weeks of Ribault's stay. He was a wise and humane leader who realized that rudeness or force would either provoke an attack, or would scatter the natives into the interior so that the French would learn nothing of them. And he saw that there was much to observe, much to admire. The people were handsome and well built:

The most part of them cover their raynes and privy parts with fair hart's skins, painted cunningly with sundry colours, and the fore part of their body and arms painted with pretty devised works of azure, red, and black, so well and so properly done as the best painter in Europe could not amend it. The women have their bodies

77

covered with a certain herb like unto moss, whereof the cedar trees and all other trees be always covered. The men for pleasure do always trim themselves therewith, after sundry fashions. They be of tawny colour, hawk nosed and of a pleasant countenance. The women be well favoured and modest and will not suffer that one approach them too near.

Though they had few tools and few weapons other than the bow and arrow, they were skilful cultivators and fishermen, built light, elegant houses of wood covered with reeds, and decorated and embellished their belongings with great artistry. Above all they appeared to lead the good life, loosely organized, independent—great runners, swimmers, shooters, preferring games to war, and leisure to work.

If the hope of ease and happiness did not draw men to such a colony, then the familiar desire for riches would take them there. From the moment of landing Ribault's expedition was on the lookout for sources of treasure. The first inquiry of the Indians, by signs and mimicry, was the whereabouts of Cibola, in northern Mexico, where there was 'great abundance of gold and silver, precious stones and other great riches' and where 'the people head their arrows, instead of iron, with pointed turquoises'. The Indians made it known that Cibola was twenty days journey by boat, but the French were soon heartened by other riches nearer at hand. They observed a native 'that had a pearl hanging at a collar of gold and silver about his neck as great as an acorn at the least' and they thought 'that there be as many as fair pearls found there as in any country in the world'. The existence of one sort of treasure gave great hopes for other kinds and Ribault, on leaving, gave instructions to the settlers that the Indians were to be wooed 'that by these means they may ask and learn of them where they take their gold, copper, turquoise, and other things yet unknown unto us, by reason of the shortness of time we sojourned there'. It was his sure expectation that the mines would be revealed by the time of his return.

Nothing was better calculated to appeal to Thomas Stukeley than the thought of plunder, wealth and the easy possession of a fair land. In his disordered imagination all ambitions were possible: to play the king was not beyond a Renaissance adventurer. His spirit, said an early biographer, 'was of so high a strain that it vilified subjection (though in the highest and chiefest degree) as contemptible, aiming (as high as the moon) at not less than sovereignty.' In 1563, as the

Spanish ambassador noted, he was close to ruin; he had little to lose but debts, misery and mean employment.

By May it was known that Stukeley was preparing for a voyage to Florida with a fleet of five ships, and Alvarez de Quadra, the Spanish ambassador, followed the preparation with interest. He discovered that two ships belonged to Stukeley, the sole remnants of his wife's fortune, and the other three were chartered from London merchants. The supplies and the ordnance were provided by the royal agents and were the queen's investment in the journey, though with typical parsimony she placed the burden of this cost on one of her unfortunate subjects. Elizabeth's part in the expedition was deliberately obscure; even the efficient de Quadra could not decide whether the fleet was financed by private citizens or by the crown. The royal patent granted to Stukeley has disappeared and the official aims of the expedition are unknown; but the Spanish ambassador did not doubt, whatever the stated purpose, that this was yet another attack on the sovereignty and possessions of Spain.

These suspicions were confirmed by Stukeley himself who, in the days before sailing, made a surreptitious approach to the ambassador. Stukeley was at his usual business, sounding out the enemy for better terms, assessing the profit in a double-cross. But fearing a trap de Quadra would not be drawn and the awkward visitor departed still in mystery, but leaving the ambassador with the sure sense of an under-hand and devious work about to begin.

On 18th June the fleet set out from Limehouse with the tide, attended from the start by surmise and suspicion.

> Now, Stukeley, hoist thy sail, thy wished land to find,
> And never do regard vain talk, for words thy are but wind.

No expedition began with such doubts of success. To the enigma of its real purpose was added the enigma of its commander. No judicious person could look on such a man leading such an expedition and fail to wonder. Ribault and the French pilots, recruited for the venture in the first days of planning, disliked the enterprise the more they saw of it. For the Frenchmen, after so much care and painful effort, to hand over the tender colony to the incalculable whim of an English adventurer was clearly incredible; at Gravesend Ribault jumped ship. Luckily for Stukeley, the French navigator was captured the next morning and thrown in the Tower before he could reveal or spoil

Panorama of London, 1543, by Anthony van den Wyngaerde. The busyness of the port and the crowded streets of the City, still familiar in its outline, are contrasted with the rural habitations of the South Bank and with the emptiness of the country beyond Stepney to the north, and Bermondsey to the south. The only considerable building is the Royal Palace of Placentia just outside the village of Greenwich.

*Guildhall Library*

the English plans. Stukeley could do without Ribault whose earnest presence was an embarrassment. But he could not manage without the pilots, and he was allowed to retain these after he had posted a bond for £300 for their good conduct and safe return. The days lost on account of the Frenchmen slid into a week lost to foul weather. On 25th June, leaving his fleet still pent up in the mouth of the Thames, Stukeley went to Greenwich where the queen waited to say farewell. He took leave of her, if a good story is to be believed, with grandiloquent insolence. 'I hope', said Elizabeth, 'I shall hear from you when you are stated in your principality.' 'I will write unto you,' quoth Stukeley. 'In what language?' said the queen. He returned, 'In the style of princes: To our dear Sister.'

But perhaps the case was different. Perhaps the answer was not that of a fool with his delusions, but rather the reply of an accomplice, an acknowledgment of illicit partnership. On 30th June, William Cecil wrote in the queen's name to warn the Lord Deputy in Ireland that Stukeley with 'a number of good ships well armed and manned' had been licensed 'to pass to discover certain lands in the west towards Terra Florida'. Cecil then added a curious instruction:

> We do will and require you, that if he shall happen to come to any part of that [Irish] coast, that ye cause him and his company to be well used, and do direct him to do any exploit by land or sea with his company that you shall find and think meet to be done for our service. And if he shall also bring or send in to any port there any manner of French ships which he shall arrest to our use, we would that the same might be received, and the goods and landings therein put in inventory, and laid up in safety, until by the further proceedings of the French we shall perceive what is meet therein for us to do.

The instruction clearly meant the Lord Deputy to welcome a state pirate, for England was not at war with France and by the custom of nations French ships should have been free from English attacks.

After a week at sea in stormy weather Stukeley's squadron from London sailed into Plymouth where the two remaining ships of his expedition waited for him. There were the *Trinity Stukeley* and the *Fortune Stukeley*, the last being jointly owned with William Hawkins, a notorious thief of the ocean, which had already carried Stukeley on several piratical ventures. For a foreign observer, the coming together in Plymouth of Stukeley, the *Fortune* and the predatory Hawkins was a sure sign of bad intentions. And when the squadron unloaded the worst fears were confirmed: spices, sugar, French wines, cloth, also three wild animals, appeared on the dock, the spoils of a merchantman met on the way from London.

With plunder near and Florida very far away, with the late summer weather unusually severe and the winter coming on, the thought of the Americas was dropped for the moment. The expedition broke up in Plymouth and Stukeley was free to go his own way, at least until the start of the next season for oceanic voyages. Implying that robbery had been all along the real purpose of the expedition, Stukeley now began a vigorous search for his share of the spoils. In December word came from the English envoys in Spain that the Spaniards were furious at the piracies of the English. A French ship bound for Bilbao with Spanish linen worth 12,000 ducats had been taken, also a French warship with a Spanish cargo worth 7,000 ducats. The robbers on these occasions were not named, but it was certainly Stukeley who descended on a north Spanish port, boldly entering the harbour and taking off two French ships laden with Spanish goods to the value of 30,000 ducats. And it was also Stukeley or one of his squadron who took the *Trinity* of Zeeland and robbed it of 'linen cloths and other wares to the value of 3,000 pounds Flemish'.

The adventurer steers his passage according to the whim of time; often fortune luckily resolves the perplexities of the feckless. No one knows if Stukeley still felt a minute compulsion to see the New World; the remnant of a private dream, the hope of territory or spectacular plunder might have taken him there. A paradise is hard to resist; as long as Florida kept its fresh, innocent image there was a chance that Stukeley would sail there. But the story of the first French settlement in Port Royal followed the familiar history of early colonies, going from bad to worse; and by strange coincidence Stukeley himself played a part in the final act of the sad episode.

Ribault had left the settlers at Charlesfort under the command of an experienced soldier, one Captain Albert de la Pierria. The early days were fair. The colonists had established themselves well enough and the Indians remained friendly. When troubles came, as was inevitable with an ill-prepared band in an unfamiliar world, the Indians rescued them. When the supplies of the settlers ran low the Indians provided a share of their own stores, though they themselves were likely to go short; and when fire destroyed the French lodgings the Indians rebuilt the log house in twelve hours, 'which being ended, they returned home fully contented with a few cutting hooks, and hatchets, which they received of our men'. Though the Indians could be pleased with simple gifts, the Frenchmen were less easily satisfied among themselves. Whether it was the trial of small misfortunes, or the friction of ill-assorted characters, the colonists began to destroy their own handiwork. René de Laudonnière, the historian of the colony, made it clear that the French brought disaster upon themselves: 'The judgment of God would have it', he wrote, 'that those which could not be overcome by fire nor water, should be undone by their own selves.'

Ascribing what happened to the natural infirmity of humans, specially those 'far from their country and absent from their countrymen', Laudonnière related the end of the colony. 'Partialities and dissensions' began when a drummer called Guernache 'was very cruelly hanged by his own captain, and for a small fault'. From this time the settlers considered that the tyranny of their captain, Albert de la Pierria, was out of hand. Not only did he hang poor Guernache, but he also degraded and banished another soldier named La Chère and refused to send this exile the food that had been promised him, saying that he would be glad to hear of his death. The protesting colonists were browbeaten and insulted with 'so evil sounding speeches, that honesty forbiddeth me to repeat them'. Setting violence against violence, 'the soldiers seeing his madness to increase from day to day, and fearing to fall into the dangers of the other, resolved to kill him'. And this they did.

The murder of the leader was an admission of defeat. In guilt and shame at their act (for they saw that they were now no better than their oppressor de la Pierria) they decided to abandon the colony, a decision that was made easier for them by the failure of Ribault to send reinforcements. Under a new commander they began to build a small pinnace, and though they had no shipwrights among them, 'necessity, which is the mistress of all sciences, taught them the way to build it'. Even then their trials were not finished; though they had a hull, they had nothing for the furnishing of the boat, for the cordage and the sails. Once more the Indians came to their help, providing ropes for the rigging and showing how rosin and moss could be got from the woods to caulk the vessel. The ship was quickly finished and though it was towards the end of the year an inviting wind persuaded them to set to sea. 'But being drunken with the too excessive joy, which they had conceived for their returning into France, or rather deprived of all foresight and consideration, without regarding the inconstancy of the winds, which change in a moment, they put themselves to sea, and with so slender victuals, that the end of their enterprise became unlucky and unfortunate.'

Having gone no more than a third of the way home they ran into calms which lasted for three weeks. Despite severe rations, the food quickly went, 'and they had nothing for their more assured refuge but their shoes and leather jerkins which they did eat'. Some drank sea water and some drank their own urine; 'and they remained in such desperate necessity a very long space, during the which part of them died for hunger'. Then a strong wind blew up and beat upon their burning faces, crashing the clumsy boat about until it half filled with water. Languishing eyes searched for the shore; the leather was gone and the few survivors were weakening fast. In this extremity they did what others in despair had done before them: they decided to kill one to save the others, and the choice fell on that same La Chère whose ill-treatment by de la Pierria had helped to start the mutiny in Florida. He was executed and his flesh was divided equally among the others, 'a thing so pitiful to recite, that my pen is loth to write it'.

Drifting at last within sight of the long-awaited shores of Europe, too far gone to manage their half-submerged wreck of a ship, the survivors of Charlesfort met a small English barque which sent men aboard, one of whom spoke to them in French. The English ship was Stukeley's, and the Frenchman was the pilot for the Florida voyage. The fortuitous meeting so far from the goal put an end to any thought of Stukeley's kingdom in Florida. These French figures-of-death were to have been his subjects; all that remained of their dominion was a rotting, sinking boat at the mercy of the waves. He took the survivors on board and returned to England.

In November Stukeley was back in London. Four months of piracy were behind him, and his creditors and backers were calling for their accounts. What he had done with the profit was never revealed—in the usual way with Thomas Stukeley the money had quite simply vanished. The acrimonious rounds of argument and litigation, so much a part of Stukeley's life, began once more, and all plans were abandoned. There was 'too little money to follow up the enterprise, many merchants he had involved in it finding themselves grossly deceived'.

Throughout the winter the writs against Stukeley accumulated in the Admiralty Court; the new Spanish ambassador Guzman de Silva

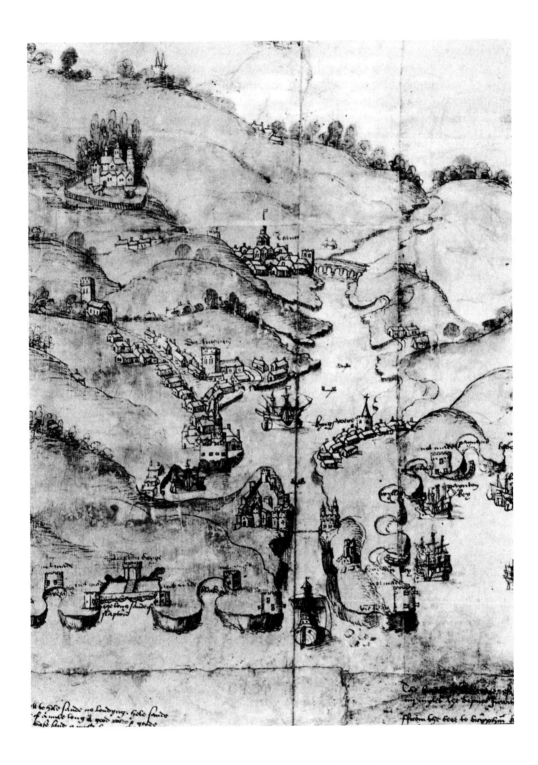

Exeter and Dartmouth harbours in the mid-sixteenth century. The small, secure harbours of the West Country were the nursery of so many notable Elizabethan seamen--adventurers, navigators and pirates.

*British Museum*

on the orders of his sovereign expressly demanded that something should be done about Stukeley; Elizabeth and Cecil were at last considering some restraint on the English pirates. The careless confusion of robbery with privateering was untangled; letters of marque were still granted to adventurers for attacks against enemy shipping, but any acts against a country with which England was officially at peace now constituted piracy, for which there were the severest penalties. London was becoming too dangerous for Stukeley and in the spring of 1564 he disappeared. And when he next came to view he was at sea once more off the coasts of the West Country and Ireland. As if for insurance, or perhaps for deceit, he still had the French pilots with him. But no one was taken in. All knew that Florida would never see him; he was back at his old game, the scourge of ships of all nations, from the French ports to Dingle Bay.

'Stukeley's piracies are much railed at here on all parts,' the English envoy wrote to Cecil from Madrid at the end of 1564. 'I hang down my head with shame enough. Alas, though it cost the Queen roundly, let him for honour's sake be fetched in. These pardons to such folk as be *hostes humani generis* I like not.' The ambassador was aware of the problem. Elizabeth had ventured on Stukeley's success and she looked for her profit. However, the outrages of the West Country pirates—Stukeley, Cobham, Frobisher, Pollard, Courtenay and a few others—grew daily more scandalous. Lord Sussex in Dublin begged Cecil 'for God's sake, employ some care' to stop 'our adventurers, that daily rob the Spaniards and Flemings'. At last instructions were given to Sir Peter Carew, a kinsman of Stukeley, to clear the pirates from the Irish coast.

Stukeley did not wait to be taken. In April 1565 he left his ship in Ireland and crossed to England to answer the charges against him. Whatever these were, they were mild enough, and Stukeley was acquitted, doubtless on the orders of high authority. In June the Lord Justice pressed for his discharge, saying that he did not understand that Stukeley 'had committed any piracy upon the coasts of Ireland or elsewhere'. Frobisher was in Launceston jail and Cobham was in the Tower (though both returned to notable exploits on the sea), but Thomas Stukeley went free. Free but not at ease, for one vital matter remained to be settled. The queen had protected him, she had supplied ammunition and stores for his use; she demanded her return with interest. But Stukeley had 'little left save his honesty'; and Elizabeth, knowing the worthlessness of that commodity, had to suffer a loss which she could never forgive. The way was prepared for Stukeley's later career: for his treason in Ireland, for his service in the papal cause, for his death at Alcazar—a knight-errant of Christendom utterly estranged from his native land, trying his desperate fortune in the hopeless crusade which Sebastian of Portugal led against the Moors. In 1583, five years after Stukeley's death, Cecil, the queen's minister, pronounced the official English verdict on him:

> Out of Ireland ran away one Thomas Stukeley, a defamed person almost through all Christendom, and a faithless beast rather than a man, fleeing first out of England for notable piracies, and out of Ireland for treacheries not pardonable.

When real intentions are so deliberately hidden, the truth is hard to reach. Authority finally abandoned Thomas Stukeley and condemned him out of hand. But he was merely a conspirator in a double-dealing policy, and his riotous excesses were only examples of deception and selfishness taken further than his partners wished. It is an open question whether the chief aim of the expedition was colonization or plunder, or if Stukeley intended to go to Florida at all. But it seems certain that Elizabeth and Cecil hoped Stukeley would combine a journey to the New World with some profitable piracy on the way. An English resident in Seville wrote to the English ambassador in Madrid after the fleet sailed from London: 'They say the Queen has delivered certain of her ships to Mr Stukeley, and he is bound to Florida with four or five ships; and to Hawkins and Cobham others, who are bound for Guinea and the Portugal Indies.' Hawkins and Cobham, as was well known, were to take their chances in the Portuguese empire, raiding, stealing, trading for their own and the queen's profit. And surely it was Elizabeth's intention that Stukeley should do the same in the New World. She had no interest in colonization as such; she needed her citizens at home for the defence of the realm. The band of Frenchmen awaiting reinforcements at Charlesfort could expect no sympathy from her.

But she was prepared to use them. If these Huguenots were ready to accept English governors, then she would send Stukeley and his men to organize the settlement into an English colony. The harbour at Port Royal would be an excellent haven from which the English adventurers could fly out against the treasure ships of the Spanish Indies. In the fortified camp at Charlesfort the spoils could be collected and guarded waiting for the return to England.

But the queen's policy did not reckon with the incalculable Thomas Stukeley. That he accepted the royal commission is easily understandable; men on the brink of ruin do not reject any lifeline, and the Indies seemed to offer unbounded possibilities. Riches and sovereignty would both attract him; no doubt in imagination he saw himself as a prince of wide acres, owner of mines, possessor of treasure, arbitrary ruler, dispenser of life and death. Ribault's portrait of a fair land encouraged dreams of power and plenitude. But Stukeley was always seduced by the chance of the moment; to wait patiently for his rewards, to plan and build, were not in his nature. Ribault was to sail with him, an anxious parent returning to his care. But Ribault and Stukeley could never have agreed on the nature of a colony––Ribault the planter, content to foster the slow growth; Stukeley the predator, stripping the land of all that it could yield. Religion also came between them. The French navigator and his Florida settlers were Protestants; but Stukeley, for all his faults, remained faithful to the old religion all his life. From that early moment, off Gravesend, when Jean Ribault leaped from the ship and out of the venture, the likelihood of a passage to Florida was very slight indeed. Everything––shipboard arguments, the queen's patent, contrary winds, the turbulence of the time, his own inclination––tempted Stukeley to concentrate on the piratical part of his commission; and Stukeley was never the man to resist a convenient temptation.

Elizabeth and Cecil should have been warned, for the sins of Stukeley were no secret. William Camden called him 'a ruffian, a riotous spendthrift, and a notable vapourer'; he had played the spy and informer at least once already, in the reign of Edward VI, and Cecil himself had examined Stukeley on that occasion; his lies were of breathtaking audacity and invention; his information had left the Council so puzzled that none of those wordly men could even hazard where the truth lay. And his approach to the Florida venture was as devious as one might expect. Before the expedition was gathered he had made advances to the Spanish ambassador. 'These people', de Quadra reported back to Spain, 'were sending him on a bad and knavish business, but he would be with me, and show me how to play them a trick to make a noise in the world.' Yet Cecil, the most cautious and knowing of ministers, protected him from the consequences of his behaviour, and still employed him.

Elizabeth arrived at her sea policy by slow steps of trial and improvisation. She understood the limitations of England. Poverty, few sources of treasure, lack of munitions, lack of an army made her extremely reluctant to test the strength of her country against the well-organized powers of Europe. In the midst of this weakness she perceived certain strengths among which was strength at sea. English ships were well-founded and the sailors active; it was a stroke of cunning to arrange matters so that the natural ambition of the sailors, greedy for wealth, would work for the benefit of England. The foreigner, worried on the seas by sudden attacks, had his trade diminished and his prosperity threatened. The Englishman who would serve his country in this way received financial backing and protection from the government; in return the queen expected a steady profit.

Such a policy relied on adventurers for its success. And no one seemed better qualified than Thomas Stukeley. The height of his ambition was only matched by the greatness of his needs. He had courage, daring and a flaunting egotism; he was an experienced commander both by land and sea. No wonder Cecil sought him out and smoothed his way. But in 1563, when she was still new to the business of ruling, Elizabeth had not yet discovered the true requirements of her policy. Stukeley lacked the essential patriotism that made robbers into heroes. Later adventurers—men like Hawkins, Drake, Raleigh or Grenville—tempered their rapacity with a Protestant and English prejudice. But Stukeley was a Catholic, and was catholic also in his crimes, as content to serve one prince as another, giving such idealism as he had left after the pursuit of his insatiable wants to the community of his fellow-Catholics rather than to England. This conduct, in an age of nationalism, made his villainy seem the more appalling, and Elizabeth and Cecil soon learnt from the error of employing him. Cecil, who had once championed him so stoutly, later wrote:

> Of this man might be written whole volumes to paint out the life of a man in the highest degree of vain-glory, prodigality, falsehood, and vile and filthy conversation of life, and altogether without faith, conscience, or religion.

Disappointment makes bitter judgments. Yet Stukeley had some unaccountable attraction that beguiled an emperor and a pope, kings and queens, dukes and archbishops, rebels and pirates alike. To Henry II of France, he was 'our dear and good friend'; Mary and Elizabeth shielded him and promoted his interests; the Duke of Savoy welcomed him; the Emperor Charles was glad to meet him. When Stukeley fled from England, Philip of Spain paid him the respect worthy of a great noble. In Rome he had more honour than any other English exile. 'It is incredible', wrote Fuller, 'how quickly he wrought himself through the notice into the favour, through the court into the chamber, yea closet, yea bosom of Pope Pius Quintus; so that some wise men thought his holiness did forfeit a parcel of his infallibility in giving credit to such a *glorioso*.' The rumour of his illegitimate royal birth perhaps helped him into the favour of princes; but, though he acted with the high-handed disdain of royalty, there is no evidence that he ever claimed royal blood. It was his character that fascinated, not his birth.

A man who was the subject, as Stukeley was, of several ballads and two large popular plays undoubtedly lived in the minds of his contemporaries. His life was a secular epic. In the fantastic vagaries of his fortune the Elizabethans saw an example of the great-hearted energy and the lust for action which they found so engaging. A churchman of the next century, when the fleeting magic of his presence was gone and only his faults were remembered, might belittle him as 'a bubble of emptiness, and meteor of ostentation', but to the Elizabethan playwright Thomas Heywood he had the spirit of a king. Or rather 'A kingdom is too small for his expense,' wrote the anonymous author of *The Life and Death of Captain Thomas Stukeley*:

> Doubtless if ever man was misbegot
> It is this Stukeley; of a boundless mind,
> Undaunted spirit, and uncontrolled spleen,
> Lavish as is the liquid Ocean,
> That drops his crowns even as the clouds drop rain.

The admiring men of his age glossed over his faults. The pursuit of 'honour', of great and singular works, challenged all morality and fate:

> honour is the thing
> Stukeley doth thirst for, and to climb the mount
> Where she is seated, gold shall be my footstool.

To live greatly was to dare all; only cowardice and a mean spirit were contemptible; death was merely the proof of a grand resolution:

> He soonest loseth that despairs to win;
> But I have no such prejudicial fear.
> If there be any shall outlive the brunt
> Of raging war, or purchase dignity,

I am persuaded to be one of those.
If all miscarry, yet it will not grieve,
Or grieve the less to die with company.

Action was its own virtue; a great attempt was worth a great reputation.

Monarchs and subjects alike saw an image of the time in this proud, engaging, brave and perilous rogue. Though eventually he earned the displeasure of the queen, he was in most ways the archetype of the Elizabethan seaman. And for the rest of her reign Elizabeth relied on adventurers like Stukeley, men as bold, ambitious and independent, but with more patriotism. No policy could have held less promise for the future of English colonization. The temper of mind of the Elizabethan adventurer was quite unsuitable for the quiet, patient work of establishing a colony. Harvesting the toil of others was his way, not the laborious planting. Impediments of thought and practice blocked the path of English colonists who followed after Sir Thomas Stukeley.

5

HONI SOIT QVI MALY PENSE

POSVI TOREIA
DEVM MEVM
ADIV

ELIZABETA D·G·ANGLIÆ·FRANCIÆ·HIBERNIÆ·ET VERGINIÆ
REGINA CHRISTIANAE FIDEI VNICVM PROPVGNACVLVM

*Immortalis honos Regum, cui non tulit ætas*      *Queis ipsa tantum superant reliqua omnia regna,*
*Ulla prior, veniens nec feret ulla parem,*      *Quantum tu maior Regibus es reliquis*

148.

Elizabeth I, 'Queen, by the grace of God, of England, France, Ireland and
Virginia'.

A woman and child of Pomeiooc,
drawn by John White. The
woman wears typical dress and
uses both beads and tattooing
for decoration. She is carrying
a water-gourd. The child holds
a doll clothed in the English
style.

*British Museum*

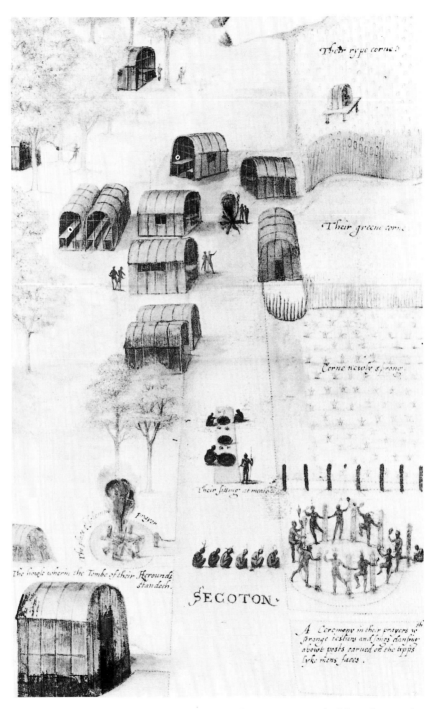

'Their towns that are not enclosed with poles are commonly fairer than such as are enclosed—compare Pomeiooc. For the houses are scattered here and there, and they have gardens wherein groweth tobacco, which the inhabitants call Uppowoc. They also have groves wherein they take deer, and fields wherein they sow their corn.' This drawing of Secoton is by John White.

*British Museum*

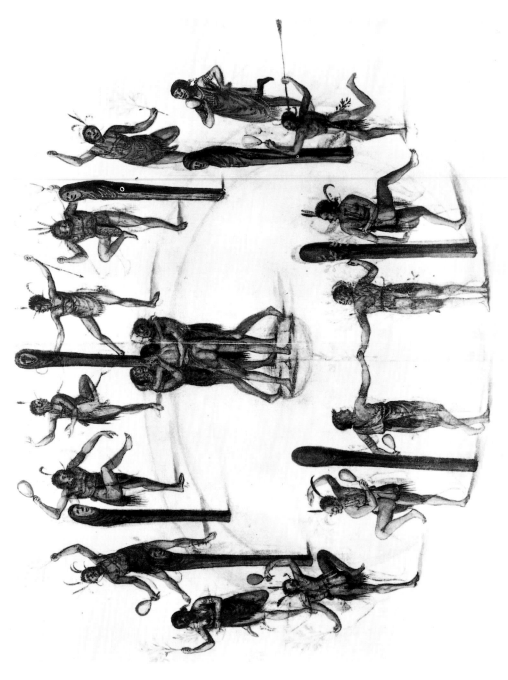

An Indian festival, probably a harvest festival, drawn by John White. 'At a certain time of the year they make a great and solemn feast . . . every man attired in the most strange fashion they can devise. Then being set in order they dance, sing, and use the strangest gestures. . . . Three of the fairest virgins of the company are in the midst, which embracing one another do as it were turn about in their dancing.'

*British Museum*

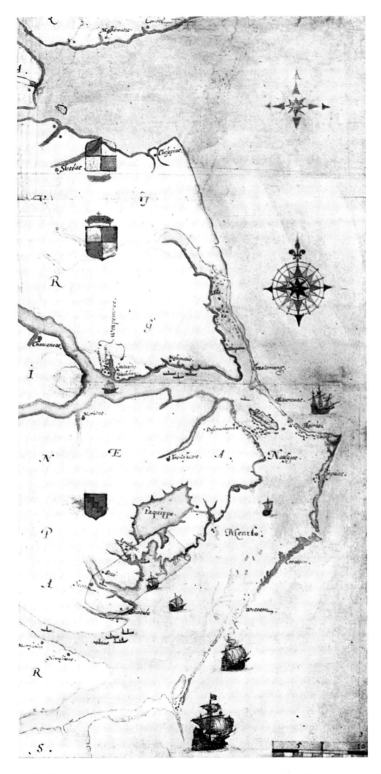

John White's map of the North American coast from Cape Lookout to Chesapeake Bay. This drawing is the most important authority on the configuration and topography of the Carolina coast in the late sixteenth century, and on the names and position of villages.

*British Museum*

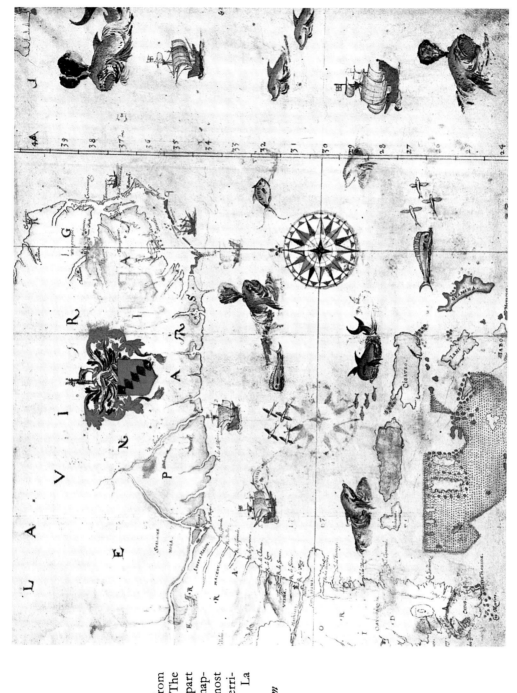

The North American coast from Florida to Chesapeake Bay. The geography of the southern part is very defective but the map-maker, John White, is most concerned with Raleigh's terri-tories in the area marked La Virgenia Pars. *British Museum*

John White's drawing of plantain. Part of White's duty was to record the flora and fauna of the New World, and this he conscientiously did. A Spaniard in Puerto Rico noted that the English 'took away with them many banana plants, and other fruits which they found along the coast, and made sketches of fruits and trees'.

*British Museum*

Platano or Plantan

A Loggerhead Turtle. This is the only sea-turtle that breeds on the Carolina Banks. The drawing is by John White.

*British Museum*

John White's drawing of a Hoopoe.

*British Museum*

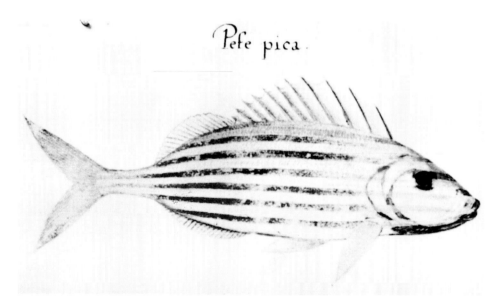

Pefe pica.

The Blue-striped Grunt of the West Indies, drawn by John White.

*British Museum*

# 5

# The Attempt of
# Sir Humphrey Gilbert

*He is not worthy to live at all, that for fear, or danger of death, shunneth his country's service, and his own honour.*

FLORIDA offered no encouragement to prudent men, for the fatal history of the colony did not end with the ocean sufferings of the first settlers. Before the few wretched skeletons who survived the flight could bring the story of their privations back to France, three ships under René de Laudonnière sailed for the relief of Port Royal. The new colonists, re-establishing the ground of the old settlement, also in a short time compounded the old mistakes, their ignorance and conceit leading to failure and early death. Laudonnière was welcomed by the Indians, but soon meddled unwisely between rival chieftains and earned nothing but distrust by his intervention. Disagreement and jealousy once more split the colonists. The Frenchmen preferred piracy to cultivation and were forced to rely on the Indians for their food, which was taken under the threat of the sword. The arrival of John Hawkins, cruising up the coast after a slaving expedition to the Spanish Indies, brought unexpected relief; he sold the colonists wine, biscuits and a ship, and with these the French determined to return to Europe. They pulled down the defences of Charlesfort, razed their huts, slaughtered the few remaining stock animals, and prepared for another flight.

In the loneliness of their distant state sudden hope alternated with more persistent despair. In the summer of 1565, when de Laudonnière was at the point of leading his men away, Jean Ribault, the father of the colony, having escaped from the labyrinth of English policy and re-formed an expedition in France, appeared off Port Royal with a squadron of seven ships. The joy and the congratulations among the

97

French were short-lived. For hardly had the French ships anchored in the estuary when the ominous sails of Spain came out of the dawn gloom: Pedro de Menendez with a fleet of thirty-four vessels and over six thousand men had come to claim the whole of Florida as the territory of the Spanish king.

The very presence of such a large force intimidated the French. Those ships of Ribault that had not yet landed took off and disappeared. With satisfaction Menendez withdrew some miles to the south and set up a base at a place he called St Augustine, destined to become the first permanent Spanish settlement north of the Gulf of Mexico, and from there he planned the destruction of the French. Hoping that surprise and determination would compensate for a weak force, Ribault decided to take all but the sick from Charlesfort and attack the Spanish by sea. But as soon as he left the shelter of the harbour a storm caught his squadron and drove the scattered ships beyond all hope of an attack. Meanwhile Menendez had decided to take Charlesfort by land, and guided by a French deserter led a strong party through swamp and forest to the helpless colony. They arrived on a night of the storm so wild that even the French watchmen had left their posts. In the confusion of the assault a few of the French escaped, but most were taken. The women and children were spared; the men were put to the sword and then hung in the trees with a notice on each man's breast declaring that he had been killed 'Not as a Frenchman, but as a Lutheran'. Afterwards, the Spaniards began a hunt for survivors which few escaped. Ribault was captured among his shipwrecked men, and murdered. It was said that his skull divided in four parts was displayed at the corners of St Augustine fort, and his beard sent as a trophy to the king of Spain.

The Spanish were formidable colonists, pressing their claims with ample power and good generalship, with practised and calculated cruelty. The division of the new discoveries by Pope Alexander VI at the end of the last century had given them the Americas as their playground, and though they might tolerate other European powers in the barren north, any attempt to settle in the warm latitudes of the east coast was seen as a challenge to their rights and a threat to their safety in the Indies. Any foreigner going there, and especially any Protestant (as the massacre of the Huguenots at Port Royal proved), was in danger. The chances of English colonization—the poorly manned, badly financed ventures of a Protestant land, with questionable aims and under devious leadership—seemed worst of all.

But the nature of the adventurer embraces danger. In 1563, while Stukeley was preparing his ships for the Florida passage, another English soldier from the West Country was at Havre in France, one of an English party sent to help the Huguenots of the Channel port. The campaign was undistinguished and boring; the plague was a greater peril than the enemy. The Englishman with a taste for exploration had time to talk and learn. Very likely he met André Thevet, a geographer who had been in the New World; certainly he met Richard Eden, translator of the *Decades*, writer on discovery and supporter of colonization. He heard of the French achievements, of the attempts at settlement on the St Lawrence by Jacques Cartier and Roberval, and in particular of the Huguenot colonies established by Villegagnon in Brazil and so recently founded by Ribault in Florida. The contemplation of the deeds of others fired his own national and Protestant pride, and a year after Ribault's murder he wrote to persuade his own country of the advantages of exploration and colonization, undeterred by the fate of Ribault, or the shameful example of Stukeley, or the grim presence of Menendez. The *Discourse of a Discovery for a New Passage to Cataia* by Humphrey Gilbert, written in 1566, announced a new and fearless champion of English expansion.

An idealism thwarted by deficient education had made Humphrey Gilbert the constant servant of nationalism. He was born shortly after Henry VIII had reformed the English church and state in the mid-thirties, and he grew up amid perplexities of religion and policy. He came from a prosperous Devon family, and though his father died young (by his mother's re-marriage Humphrey had the famous Sir Walter Raleigh as a half-brother) he was given the best schooling, going from Eton to Oxford. But his schooling was pedantic and old-fashioned, a dull Latin drudgery that seemed to have no relevance to the difficulties of the age. Gilbert did not consider that a correct knowledge of Latin, some sprinklings of ancient culture, and a facility in French and Spanish were the ends of education; in later life he wrote a work on education called *Queen Elizabethes Achademy* in which he spoke of rich youths being 'obscurely drowned in education'. The young, he complained in the same work, were 'estranged from all serviceable virtues to their prince and country'.

Fortunately for his ardent Protestant mind, this ignorance of the proper affairs of his country was relieved through the intervention of one of his relatives. His aunt, Katherine Ashley, was the governess and friend of young Princess Elizabeth, and in 1555, when the princess

QVID NON:

VIRGINIA

Sr Humphry Gilbert knight

Heere may yee see the pourtraict of his face
Who for his countries honour oft did trace
Along the deepe, and made a noble way
Vnto our growing fame Virginia
The picture of his minde if yee do craue it
Looke vpon vertues picture and yee haue it

Sir Humphrey Gilbert. The inscription in the upper left—*Quid Non*—was Gilbert's motto, and expressed very well his impatient and speculative mind.

was finally cleared of complicity in Wyatt's rebellion, Humphrey Gilbert joined the princess's household at Hatfield. Here his gallant and handsome presence made a mark with the witty Elizabeth: 'Her Majesty', wrote the chronicler John Hooker, 'had a special good liking to him, and very oftentimes would familiarly discourse and confer with him in matters of learning.' And Elizabeth, only some four years older but many ages wiser than young Gilbert, found an apt pupil in her courtier. He began his education in 'serviceable virtue' to prince and country. His experience in these years made him the queen's man, and he ached to do some notable work to advance the cause of his country and his sovereign. 'O noble prince,' he wrote to her in *Queen Elizabethes Achademy*, 'that God shall bless so far as to be the only mean of bringing this seely, frozen Island into such everlasting honour that all the nations of the world shall know and say, when the face of an English gentleman appeareth, that he is either a soldier, a philosopher, or a gallant courtier.' Instructed by the young princess, Gilbert became a Protestant patriot for the mature queen to use. He had served Elizabeth, he wrote at the end of his life, 'in wars and peace, above seven and twenty years . . . from a boy to the age of white hairs'.

Ambition and a courtly training made a soldier of Gilbert, but all his life, in the midst of armies, he heard a distant sound of the sea. The memories of childhood by Dartmouth harbour, the voyages, trials, storms, piracies of his many Devon relatives, marked an impressionable mind. Always in the intervals between the campaigns he turned to thoughts of ocean voyages. At Havre, conversation with navigators and historians made him aware of how much had been done in the way of exploration, and how little England had as yet contributed. He returned from France anxious for the honour of his country and luckily discovered, in the late summer of 1564, a land ready to take a stronger part in discovery. Thomas Stukeley was even then at sea supposedly bound for Florida. Anthony Jenkinson returned in September with land trade from the Middle East on behalf of the Muscovy Company. Argument broke out in England once more concerning travel and trade, how the riches of the Far East were to be reached. Gilbert set himself to study geography, navigation and the history of discovery.

Jenkinson was not satisfied with the overland journeys of the Muscovy Company. They had led to some trade with Russia and Persia, but the far eastern goal of all desires—Japan and the Spice Islands—was still too far away. He wished to try a sea-route as Willoughby, Chancellor and Borough, the first captains of the Company, had done some ten years before. 'I am persuaded', he petitioned the queen in May 1565, 'that . . . there is no doubt of a passage to be found.' Like his predecessors, he favoured a north-east passage to the north of Russia, but he admitted another possibility, for some believed in a voyage by the north-west '(taking their authority of certain authors who wrote by conjecture) which opinion I do not wholly dissent from'.

Gilbert had looked into 'the authors who wrote by conjecture', making little distinction between the mythologists and the sober geographers, between Plato and Ortelius, and his studies had convinced him of the advantages of the north-west passage. He also petitioned the queen: 'Whereas of long time, there has been nothing said or done concerning the discovery of a passage by the North, to go to Cataia, and all other the east parts of the world,' he would undertake such a journey with his brothers at their own expense so long as they were granted certain rights and trading monopolies. Jenkinson and Gilbert argued the virtues of their respective routes before Elizabeth and the Council, relying on such evidence as the discovery of the unicorn's horn in the north of Russia; the debate must have revealed more ignorance than knowledge, for soon after the two contenders decided to pool their resources and arrange a joint expedition. When Jenkinson returned to Russia for the Muscovy Company in May 1566, Gilbert set about his *Discourse*, giving a full and persuasive case for a north-west passage.

The *Discourse* proposed to give substance to dreams, to chart a practical course to the land of desire. Gilbert wrote to his brother John:

> Sir, you might justly have charged me with an unsettled head if I had at any time taken in hand, to discover Utopia, or any country fained by imagination: But Cataia [China] is none such, it is a country, well known to be described and set forth by all modern Geographers, whose authority in this art (contrary to all other) beareth most credit, and the passage thereunto, by the Northwest from us, through a sea which lieth on the Northside of Labrador, mentioned and proved, by no small number of the most expert, and best learned amongst them.

The *Discourse*, though full of puzzling misinformation and fanciful deductions, was the first important document of the Elizabethan age on exploration and voyaging. The points of Gilbert's treatise become the pre-occupation of English sea policy. He spoke of the riches to be found, of the increase of royal power, of the benefits to English trade and to English shipping, and of outflanking Spain and Portugal in the

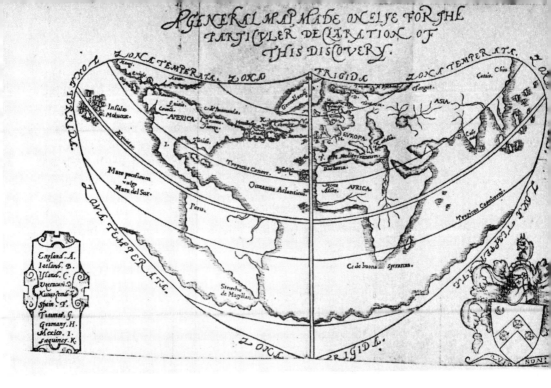

World map by Humphrey Gilbert, printed in his *Discourse*, 1576. This is a conjectural map, not based on any actual voyage, illustrating Gilbert's general thesis and hopefully showing a north-west passage to the Indies and Japan. Gilbert was not able to correct his map from experience; his 'cardes and plots' went down with him in the *Squirrel*.

rush for treasure. He gave a form and a voice to much that had been discussed among small circles of scholars and sailors for many years past. Nothing in the *Discourse* was new, but certain suggestions had a bearing on the future. English navigators were once more turned towards the north-west passage, the special territory of the English since the early days of Sebastian Cabot but lately neglected owing to the partial success of the Muscovy Company in the north-east. Also, the *Discourse* put forward the possibility of colonization:

> We might inhabit some part of those countries, and settle there such needy people of our country, which now trouble the common wealth, and through want here at home, are inforced to commit outrageous offences, whereby they are dayly consumed with the gallows.

The *Discourse* was written for Gilbert's own benefit, to set his own thoughts in order and to appease his elder brother, the head of the family, to whom 'this voyage seemed strange and had not been commonly spoken of before'. Gilbert was contemplating a voyage with Jenkinson, but there was no sign that he proposed to found a colony; the short passage on colonization in the *Discourse* was only a part of a general argument, showing that a settlement could help trade and give a relief to certain social problems at home. As a speculative adventurer, Gilbert no doubt saw little profit for himself in colonial ventures. It needed Ireland to teach him that colonies gave their masters riches and power.

Whatever Gilbert might intend, it was the queen who ruled his fortunes. Before his plans for a sea voyage to the north-west had a chance to mature he was sent to the Irish wars, arriving there in July 1566. The English faced serious trouble in Ireland. Most of the country was aflame, fanned by the successful rebellion of Shane O'Neill in Ulster. Against this turmoil the English placed both a campaign of terror and a policy of colonization. And Humphrey Gilbert, in the four years of his Irish service, had a conspicuous part in both aspects of English policy. The purpose of the English soldiers, as Sir Henry Sidney, the Lord Deputy of Ireland, expressed it, was to make the name of Englishman 'more terrible now to them than the sight of a hundred was before'—a policy which Gilbert supported well. Within a short time of landing in Derry, Gilbert had learnt to practise the habitual bestiality of Irish warfare. In three years he rose to be colonel in command of the forces in Munster.

'That authority', he wrote to Cecil on appointment to his command, 'was to me but a sweet poison, that would in the end turn to my confusion and utter discredit, rather than to the increase of my poor reputation.' His conduct won the applause of his government, but the disgust of posterity. Heads tumbled, bodies of women and children bordered the roads, the fields were devastated so that famine and disease broke those spared by the swords:

> They looked like anatomies of death; they spoke like ghosts crying out of their graves; they did eat the dead carrions, happy when they could find them; yea they did eat one another soon after, inasmuch as the very carcasses they spared not to drag out of their graves.

In December 1569 Gilbert sent an account of his methods to Cecil in London. He would not parley with rebels nor give any quarter to those, friends or family, who supported them, 'putting also all those from time to time to the swords that did belong, feed, accompany, or maintain any outlaws or traitors'. If a castle or fort would not yield, he 'would not afterward take it of their gift but win it perforce, how many lives so ever it cost, putting man, woman, and child of them to the sword, neither did I spare any malefactor unexecuted that came into my hands in any respect. . . . Being for my part constantly of this opinion that no conquered nation will ever yield willingly their obedience for love but rather for fear'. Observers confirmed the effect of this resolute cruelty. 'His manner', wrote Thomas Churchyard in his *General Rehearsal of Wars* (1579), 'was that the heads of all those (of what sort so ever they were) which were killed in the day should be cut off from their bodies, and brought to the place where he encamped at night, and should there be laid on the ground by each side of the way leading into his own tent, so that none could come into his tent but commonly he must pass through a line of heads, which he used *ad. terrorem.*'

It is no wonder that the Irish—as one of his officers reported—accounted Gilbert 'more like a devil than a man, and are so afraid of him that they did leave and give up twenty-six castles'. His conduct had the enthusiastic approval of authority. 'For the Colonel,' Sidney wrote to Cecil, 'I cannot say enough.' He had made the highways safe and the towns free; he had destroyed the traitors, 'the arch-rebel James FitzMaurice only excepted, who is become a bush-beggar, not having twenty knaves to follow him'; he had made the English formidable, and filled the hearts of the Irish with fear. And for all this, the Lord Deputy concluded: 'I had nothing to present him with but the honour of knighthood, which I gave him; for the rest I recommend him to your friendly support.'

Efficient, cruel, Gilbert laid waste Ireland with a kind of savage contempt—certainly for his enemy, perhaps also for himself, that he should be put to such work. Many times he tried to escape. He was ill; he complained of trouble with his eyes. He returned hopefully to England from time to time and was sent back to Ireland. He tried to press forward with his plans for a sea voyage to the north-west passage. In December 1566 he petitioned the queen for 'licence and favour to enterprise and give the attempt with all possible speed for the discovery of a passage to Cataia and all other the rich parts of the world as yet unfound, which taking good success shall be great honour and strength to your majesty with immortal fame throughout all the world'. Elizabeth was never deceived by outrageous promises; she asked for a report on the project from the Muscovy Company, and the powerful

This scene, though not taken from Gilbert's campaigns, was typical of the incessant Irish warfare of late Tudor times. The English, forcing a crossing of the Erne against the opposition of Hugh Maguire, cause great carnage among the Irish by reason of numerous cavalry and superior fire-power. 'The musketeers in the woods bordering on the river shot down with impunity the Catholics who stood in the open.'

*British Museum*

London merchants of the Company, anxious to retain the monopoly of far distant trade, answered unfavourably. Blocked on this road, Gilbert turned towards thoughts of colonization in Ireland. English plantation in Ireland, as a means to quell the disaffected land, had been tried before, in the shadow of the Pale around Dublin; and when Gilbert arrived in 1566 Sir Henry Sidney was ready to try the experiment in Ulster. How Humphrey Gilbert was brought into the scheme is not known, but a man who had already suggested the colonization of the New World would be naturally interested in colonies so much nearer home.

Early in 1567 Gilbert was on leave from Ireland looking among his Devonshire friends for partners in an Irish venture. The queen approved plantation 'so by continuance of time to stablish those countries with English birth and government', and took note, writing to Sidney in July, that 'our servant Humphrey Gilbert is instructed from certain gentlemen in the west parts here to deal with you in this behalf'. In the same month the vice-chamberlain, Sir Francis Knollys, suggested that Gilbert should be made president of a new settlement. Nothing came of this plan, for the difficulties of settling in a mutinous state had been underestimated. The business of settlement was liable to be expensive and could only succeed if private speculators saw an attractive return. Yet at first view the expense outweighed all profit; settlers, as Sidney told Cecil, 'must be so furnished with money, apparel, victual, and means to till the ground, and indeed little else shall they find saving only flesh, and some beasts for caring of the ground'. Gilbert and his colleagues began to seek an adequate return.

When duty took Gilbert from Ulster to Munster, he transferred his hopes for a settlement to the south and west of Ireland. Grenville and St Leger, two adventurers from the west of England, had bought land near Cork from the Anglo-Irish Desmond family. Unable to settle this territory themselves, they invited Gilbert and some others to help with a plantation of Englishmen around Baltimore, to the west of Cork. These gentlemen at first had an eye to the fishing of the south coast which they petitioned to exploit free from all custom. By the end of 1569 this simple aim had grown into a grand scheme to possess all escheated and forfeited lands in Munster and all harbours and islands between Rosse and the Blasket Islands. They offered to build a town at Baltimore and pay a yearly rental for land and fishing rights. Great benefits would follow for England. Loyal citizens would take the place of rebel Irish; English fishermen and traders would profit; ships of other nations would be driven from Irish ports; and the 'noisome number of pirates' who lurked about the Irish coast would be discouraged. And the speculators (though they refrained from mentioning it) would grow rich from the possession of land, from the control of trade, from the farming out of licenses, and from the profits of the fishing.

The Council in London was sympathetic to a scheme which would create a little England at no cost to the crown, but wisely limited the size of the colony lest the speculators should grow too powerful. The cautious negotiations continued through 1569 until the eruption of FitzMaurice in Munster blew away the delightful dreams of easy profit. Gilbert became no longer the colonist but the avenging sword, earning his reputation as the scourge of Ireland. In January 1570, the worst of his work completed, he hurried from Ireland and strongly resisted attempts to get him back though the government very likely intended Gilbert, and not Sir John Perrot, to be the first president of Munster. Conscience or disgust made him pursue his scheme at a distance from the land that he had devastated. Perrot ruled in Munster while Gilbert devised further colonial plans in the safety of England. In 1572 Gilbert and his uncle were once more trying to found a colony in County Cork. All his plans came to nothing; English ambition, English greed were overcome by the desperation of an angry land.

Four years in Ireland gave Humphrey Gilbert an enduring reputation for ruthless ferocity. In 1581 his half-brother Raleigh, then serving in Munster, wrote: 'Would God the service of Sir Humphrey Gilbert might be rightly looked into, who with the third part of the garrison now in Ireland ended a rebellion not much inferior to this in two months. . . . I never heard or read of any man more feared than he is among the Irish nation.' In an age of savage killings the hardness of the man was unremarkable; his contemporaries admired his resolution and efficiency. The Irish could expect no mercy from him. He was put to great expense by his military duties, for in the manner of Elizabeth's commanders he was forced to support his campaign out of his own pocket; he left Ireland being owed the large sum of £3315 7s. His plans for colonies were in part attempts to make good his loss, and it was in his interest to exploit the country of his enemy as much as he could. Moreover, the ardour of his nationalism gave him a contempt for all other people; the requirements of English policy overrode all rights. He swept aside the liberties of the Anglo–

Sir John Hawkins at the age of 63, by the exiled Flemish painter Hieronimo Custodis.

*City of Plymouth Museum and Art Gallery*

Irish, 'answering them that the Prince had a regular and absolute power, and that which might not be done by the one I would do by the other in cases of necessity'. The native Irish he viewed as nothing more than beasts: 'He thought his dogs' ears too good to hear the speech of the greatest noble man amongst them.' There is no blindness like that of an idealist, no oppression crueller than that of a patriot.

The qualities that made him feared gave him also a distinction of another kind. He had supported the peaceful cause of exploration with the same imagination and singlemindedness that he gave to war, and won a reputation as a cosmographer and navigator before he had ever made a long sea voyage. Then as now persistent talk often outweighed silent performance. In 1567 the Spanish ambassador thought it necessary to warn his master of Gilbert: 'There is here an English gentleman, as they say, a great cosmographer, who thinks he has found a way, shorter than that which the Portuguese make, for the east India.' Four years later Dr John Dee, scientist and astrologer, found in Gilbert the spirit of discovery that should serve as an example to his countrymen. 'Thereof, verily, might grow commodity, to this land chiefly, and to the rest of the Christian commonwealth, far passing all riches and worldly treasure.' If England was not yet persuaded, Gilbert at least intended to realise the high hopes of Dee. And the attempts at settlement in Ireland suggested to him a new use for the American wilderness.

'He is not worthy to live at all', Gilbert had written in his *Discourse*, 'that for fear, or danger of death, shunneth his country's service and his own honour.' He still wished his own achievement to be for the glory of queen and country, but even patriotic ambition had to wait on time. In 1571 Gilbert entered Parliament, he and John Hawkins being elected for the town of Plymouth. In the Commons his worship of the crown, in particular his defence of the royal prerogative, earned him the enmity of parliamentarians. Peter Wentworth, the boldest of the Parliament men, 'noted his disposition to flatter and fawn on the Prince, comparing him to the chameleon, which can change himself into all colours, saving white; even so (said he) this reporter can change himself into all fashions but honesty'. He received a profitable sinecure for his service. The years brought prosperity. He married a wife who would bear him seven children. He held positions in his native Devonshire and could not avoid being called back to the wars, taking part (together with his young half-brother Walter Raleigh) in a small, ignoble campaign in the Netherlands. But his speculative mind was not tied down by affairs. He tried alchemy and lost money; he wrote his little book on education and a treatise on Ireland. In the winter of 1575 the poet George Gascoigne visited Gilbert at his house in Limehouse and found a man at work among his schemes: 'And being very bold to demand of him how he spent his time in this loitering vacation from martial stratagems, he courteously took me up into his study, and there shewed me sundry profitable and very commendable

This impressive portrait of Martin Frobisher, painted by the Dutch artist Cornelius Ketel, was one of a series of pictures commissioned by the Cathay Company to celebrate Frobisher's voyage of 1577.
*The Bodleian Library, Oxford*

exercises, which he had perfected painfully with his own pen.'

Sounds of the port penetrated that study at Limehouse; the masts of ships made long shadows on the waterfront houses. The old enthusiasm for the sea, so long laid aside for war and business, crept back to Gilbert's mind. He was once more in conversation with captains and navigators. Frobisher and Michael Lok were planning an attempt on the north-west passage for the Muscovy Company, and in 1575 Lok and Gilbert discussed the project together, though Gilbert (as Lok admitted) had little of value for such an old hand as Michael Lok. Gascoigne, a relative of Frobisher, was one of the group, and his inquisitive ferreting among Gilbert's papers brought out the *Discourse* of many years before which Gascoigne carried off in triumph to the press in 1576. The *Discourse* made a small stir among speculators and sailors alike. It helped to give an air of respectability and learning to Frobisher's voyages to the north-west, even when that venture fell from its high exploratory purpose and became, in 1577–8, an undignified gold rush. The ore which Frobisher found was not gold but pyrites, fit for nothing except 'to mend the highways'; yet when the detractors of Frobisher muttered, the poet Churchyard reproached them for lack of faith, seeing that Gilbert and other 'very grave and honourable personages do set their helping hands to the same'.

The drift of affairs took England into more active opposition to Spain. Elizabeth would not risk outright war, but she encouraged the spoiling of the Spanish empire by English adventurers. In 1572 Drake led the way to the riches of the Caribbean, and others soon followed. In 1576 John Oxenham set out to make a raiding base in Panama; after many vicissitudes he was marooned in Peru without ships but with plenty of treasure. The clandestine preparations for Drake's world voyage were going on in England, and he left, amid much secrecy, towards the end of 1577. It seemed that all the deep-sea sailors were on the water with plans of piracy, trade or exploration. Gilbert alone appeared to be landlocked. He who was the loudest champion of sea enterprise saw others gather the riches and the fame. In August 1577 the Council learnt that Gilbert was in his native Devon 'ready to cross sails'. But no one was sure what he intended; rumour had it that he was bound for Peru to relieve Oxenham 'that hath £150,000 in gold but he hath no shipping nor means to bring it thence'. The rumour doubtless reveals some uncertainty in Gilbert's mind, desperate to get to sea, drawn to an imaginative and arduous venture, eager for treasure, and anxious to serve England. But he needed the queen's permission to make a voyage, and looked for ways to obtain it.

The stir of animosity against Spain, which was supported by Gilbert's belligerent nationalism, gave him the key. In November 1577 he addressed Elizabeth in two documents both entitled 'How Her Majesty May Annoy the King of Spain'. Gilbert proposed to fit out an expedition which, under cover of 'some colourable means: as by giving of licence under letters patent to discover and inhabit some strange place', would seize and despoil the Newfoundland fishing fleets of Spain, Portugal and France. The capture of these fishing vessels would weaken the commerce and reduce the ships of England's enemies. And when this was done, Gilbert further suggested that another fleet should sail, pretending 'to inhabit St Lawrence Island [possibly Anticosti], the late discovered countries in the North, or elsewhere', but in reality to creep down the coast for an assault on the Spanish Indies, then to take Santo Domingo and Cuba, making them into fortified English colonies and bases for the future destruction of the Spanish empire. All this deception was licensed, he wrote, by both religion and policy; his country's good (as he had said in Ireland) sanctified most sins: 'I hold it as lawful in Christian policy, to prevent a mischief betime, as to revenge it too late, especially seeing that God himself is a party in the common quarrels now afoot, and his enemy's malicious disposition towards your Highness, and his Church, manifestly seen.' Once more a confusion of purpose: a use for colonization was dimly perceived, but what was the value of a colony—a cloak for war, a stronghouse for plunder, an adjunct to aggressive policy?

The scheme was too bold, and likely to be too expensive, for the queen. Delays, indecision, the moderating hand of time blurred the outline of the first concept. Though the details are not recorded, some plans went forward in which thoughts of colonization fluctuated with the desire for spoils. The lawyer Richard Hakluyt, uncle of the famous historian of the same name, prepared some notes on colonization which were probably intended for Gilbert's use. These notes contemplated peaceful settlement rather than a colony of warriors, and abounded in practical good sense. Hakluyt recommended a place by the seaside, 'in temperate climate in sweet air, where you may possess always sweet water, wood, sea-coals or turf, with fish, flesh, grain, fruits, herbs, and roots'. He spoke of mines, and cultivation, and harbours, and trade. He suggested even that imperial ambition was unnecessary for successful settlement, that a small enclave surrounded by 'savages' would have advantages: 'Yet if we might enjoy traffic and be assured of the same', he wrote, 'we might be much enriched, our navy might be increased, and a place of safety might there be found, if change of religion or civil wars should happen in this realm, which are things of great benefit.'

It seems that the peaceful advice of Hakluyt had to contend with the familiar instincts of adventurers. In the spring of 1578 the Spanish ambassador Mendoza repeatedly warned his master of English plans in which the coming expedition of Gilbert figured large. Gilbert, wrote Mendoza, had 'four ships on this coast bought with his own resources and very well armed'; his aim was to land on the island of 'Santa Genela'. In June, Mendoza had a more circumstantial story: Gilbert was to join in a venture against the Indies and for that purpose had hired a pilot, 'one Simon Fernandez, a Portuguese, a thorough-paced scoundrel, who has given and is giving them much information about that coast, which he knows very well'. It was the English opinion, Mendoza reported, 'that the way to insure themselves against your Majesty and put a stop to your good fortune was to make a course to the Indies and rob the fleets, unless they could establish a footing on the coast, for thus they would prevent so much money coming to your Majesty'. The astute ambassador perceived the springs of English policy, and knew that colonization was but a part of a larger strategy.

On 11th June 1578 the queen granted letters patent to Sir Humphrey Gilbert 'to discover search find out and view such remote heathen and barbarous lands countries and territories not actually possessed by any Christian prince or people'. These lands Gilbert was 'to have hold occupy and enjoy to him his heirs and assigns forever'. Six years were given him to carry out his task, and he was granted full powers to legislate and administer for the colony as a vassal of the English crown. The fruits of settlement would be his, subject only to a royalty paid to the queen on all precious metals found in the new territory. Beyond these general provisions the patent was vague; no place was specified, though the notes of Hakluyt and also Mendoza's information suggested a destination in a warm climate, perhaps between the Spanish outposts in Florida and the Hudson River. No reason was given for the colony, though at one point the patent spoke darkly of a 'second journey for conquest'. Nor were Gilbert's preparations any more revealing than his instructions. Mendoza thought him bound for the West Indies; the French ambassador wrote confidently that the expedition was heading for 'Terra Australis Incognita' of the southern hemisphere. Lord Lincoln, the Lord Admiral, was as puzzled as the foreigners; he thought Gilbert intended 'to seek a voyage into the India'.

In close secrecy, answerable only to their own obscure dreams, the men of the expedition gathered in the West Country. 'But such that seeks for fame in foreign place, forsakes great ease, and wealth where they were bred,' wrote Thomas Churchyard, 'are special men, and do deserve more grace than all the rest.' The nature of Elizabeth's policy gave them a licence to satisfy unfathomable desires, and once launched by authority their wayward progress was ungovernable. Greed, ambition, some private passion, or the chance throw of fortune's dice brought them to Dartmouth. Among men of disdainful pride quarrels broke out. Henry Knollys, Gilbert's chief partner, would not accept a subordinate place and eventually left in his ship the *Francis*, taking two others with him. The Council viewed the gathering with apprehension, for many of the ships were armed to the teeth and some of the captains were known to be pirates. Simon Fernandez had been to gaol in Glamorgan and John Callis of the *Elephant* was well known to the commissioners for piracy in that county. In July the Council ordered a halt to the warlike preparation of the ships, but already Knollys was raiding in the Channel with some of the expedition. Departure was delayed beyond the summer season; the stores were stolen; some flew off to satisfy private business. On 26th September the full fleet of eleven ships and five hundred men sailed from Dartmouth, only to be driven back by contrary winds. In October they tried again with the same result. On 18th November, with many recriminations and the greatest ill-feeling, three pirates—Knollys of the *Francis*, Edward Denye of the *Bark Denye* and Callis of the *Elephant*—went their own way to fields of plunder, and Gilbert with the remaining ships departed next day. Sir Humphrey commanded from the *Anne Aucher*, having with him six other ships of varying size, in all 409 men and 122 guns.

They were gone, Churchyard wrote:

> But whither, no man knows,
> Save that they are in bark.

Forthright voices, knowing very well the nature of the adventurers, claimed that the force behind the expedition was 'a greedy hope of gain, And heaps of gold you hope to find'. The ships, spiky as hedgehogs with guns, looked like a raiding party; the autumn departure, too late for the waters of the north Atlantic and too late for the proper establishment of a colony before the coming of winter, suggested a fleeting visit to a warm climate. At a later date Edward Hayes, a captain in Gilbert's second expedition and the historian of that venture, wrote of the first that 'the preparation was expected to grow into a puissant fleet, able to encounter a king's power by sea'. History which is silent on the conduct of Gilbert and the main party gives a hurried glimpse of the fortunes of certain ships. Miles Morgan of the *Red Lion* joined Knollys in the capture of a French merchantman; his ship was then lost at sea and Morgan drowned. Of the queen's ship the *Falcon*, captained by Walter Raleigh, the chroniclers gave different reports. 'I seek not death, nor flee the end,' was the motto of the *Falcon* and it was said that Raleigh lived up to that high sentence, attempting a voyage to the West Indies and meeting on the way storms and battles 'when many of your company were slain, and your ships therewith also sore battered and disabled'. Another account has Raleigh abandoning his adventures 'for want of vittels and other necessaries'.

Of Gilbert's own part in the expedition there is little evidence. By April 1579 he was certainly back in England claiming a 'great loss because I would not myself, nor suffer any of my company to do anything contrary to my word given to her Majesty'. Privateer he might have been, for his instructions condoned that, but piracy he denied. The Spanish had a different view of his conduct. Mendoza wrote of Gilbert 'going about robbing' and charges were drawn up against him: he aided Morgan in the attack on the *Mary*, took Spanish goods and sold them in Cornwall; he and others of his expedition had sacked a village and despoiled a shrine on the coast of Galicia; several of his captains had committed notorious acts of piracy. The last charge was too obviously true. In April 1579 the Council temporarily revoked his patent unless he stood surety for the good behaviour of his associates. Even this mark of displeasure did not prevent the theft of a Spanish shipload of oranges actually within Dartmouth harbour. Gilbert's venture now risked 'her Majesty's indignation' and Gilbert, Raleigh and some others faced arrest. At last restitution was made for the Spanish fruit and Gilbert did his penance. In June 1579 he was sent to Ireland once more, given the expensive and wearisome task of subduing the fleet of his old enemy James FitzMaurice.

The first cast into sea adventure landed Gilbert nothing but trouble.

Six months of maritime activity left him with neither a colony nor riches. Service in Ireland once again cost him dearly; his sailors made off with two of his ships for want of wages leaving him with the *Squirrel* only, a tiny frigate of less than ten tons. His loss came to some £2,000. The unruly spirit of his colleagues and his own questionable conduct brought him under the suspicion of the government. His only assets were the grants allowed him by the patent of 1578 and he shrewdly decided to exploit these for the re-establishment of his fortunes. Colonization had been fitfully in his mind for fifteen years and more, but he had hoped, with the opportunism of his kind, to combine settlement with plunder. Privateering brought him grief and he learnt that robbing and planting are not easily reconciled. He set out on the second path, hoping that the colonies permitted by his grant would satisfy an unfulfilled ambition. Since his property was sold or mortgaged his first need was for new funds; so he granted (Edward Hayes wrote) 'certain assignments out of his commission to sundry persons of mean ability, desiring the privilege of his grant, to plant and fortify in the North parts of America about the river of Canada'. Gilbert's own intention, as Mendoza confirmed, was still to head for the warm lands, perhaps to the part of Florida where Ribault had been. But he was prepared to allow rival settlements in the north, for he retained some profitable rights over them.

The years gave Gilbert a new audience; those who might have dismissed his expansive plans in 1566 listened carefully in 1580. For England was at last fully awake to new possibilities in far-distant lands. The efforts of the voyagers began to feed the hungry imagination of the land. The three journeys of Martin Frobisher after 1576 gave a deceptive promise of gold, and the pillaging expeditions of Hawkins, Drake and other patriotic adventurers saw the accumulation of much treasure; when Drake returned from his voyage round the world, in September 1580, his vast hoard of riches is said to have paid his supporters 4,700 per cent on their investment. Gentlemen were keen to get to sea, and those that could not sail speculated on those who could. Schemes of aggression or robbery or discovery tumbled out with more enthusiasm than sense, so that the ever-watchful Mendoza had a hundred hare-brained and scarcely possible ventures to report. In January 1581 the ambassador wrote that Knollys was to winter off Brazil with six ships and then join Drake in the South Sea, 'robbing all he can'; Gilbert was to go to Cuba with another six 'and there to fortify a suitable place, sallying forth in search of any fleets that leave

English boat attacked by Eskimos, after John White. It is likely that
White made his drawings of Eskimos after Frobisher's expedition in
1577. Eskimo resistance to Frobisher's headlong attempt to plunder
their land would be perfectly understandable.

*British Museum*

either Santo Domingo or neighbouring islands as well as those of Nueva España and Peru'; Frobisher was once again to attempt the north-west passage to Cathay and the Spice Islands.

And all this planning, all the dreaming, was pressed on by a sudden spate of new books, feeding the new-found interest. After the publication of Gilbert's *Discourse* in 1576 came reports of voyages, translations of foreign adventures, books on travel, geography and navigation. Frobisher's journeys had several historians; works by Encisco, Gomara, Guevara, Monardes and Escalante were translated from the Spanish and Portuguese; works by Cartier and others were translated from French. The *History of Travel* by Richard Willes, published in 1577, continued the tale begun in Eden's *Decades* some twenty-two years previously; John Frampton translated the *Travels of Marco Polo* in 1579, and three years later the important *Arte de Navegar* of Pedro de Medina. Dr John Dee, that indefatigable man of science, produced several pieces on geography, navigation and cartography. The evidence in England, on the sea and in the study, attested to not only an inquiry after knowledge of foreign parts but also a desire to emulate others and to possess: 'The time approacheth and now is', Richard Hakluyt wrote with confident prediction in 1582, 'that we of England may share and part stakes (if we will ourselves) both with the Spaniard and with the Portugal in part of America and other regions as yet undiscovered.'

Hakluyt and England, ready for the work of settlement, were the disciples of Sir Humphrey Gilbert. His first intention, to refill his purse by assigning colonial rights, seems to have failed. The only assignment on record was inevitably to the inveterate speculator John Dee; whether or not other assignments were made, Gilbert's poverty was not eased. In July 1581 he wrote to the queen's secretary, Sir Francis Walsingham, complaining of 'daily arrests, executions, and outlawries'; he was reduced, he said, 'to gadge and sell my wife's clothes from her back'. In October he pleaded that unless he had the sums owed to him 'I should be utterly undone, not able to shew my head for debts'. He decided therefore to press on with a scheme for colonization in which others would take shares but he would play the leading part. He saw time running away, and his patent was due to expire in the summer of 1584.

Some preparation had already been done. Early in 1580 Gilbert sent Simon Fernandez with the little *Squirrel* to sound out the American coast. Fernandez, whose sailing ability made him a very valuable man despite a well-known liking for piracy, was back in Dartmouth by June, bringing the hide of an American buffalo and certain information on Indian life. Gilbert also talked with John Walker who led another expedition to the North American 'river of Norumbega' in the same year. Walker's story was encouraging: he had discovered a silver mine on the banks of a large, deep river with good navigation; the country was 'most excellent both for the soil, diversity of sweet woods and trees'; and his company had also found a native house containing three hundred dried skins 'whereof the most part of them were eighteen foot by the square'. Precious metal, fine country, profitable commodities—good baits for settlers.

On 19 April 1582 a government agent reported that 'there is a muttering among the Papists that Sir Humphrey Gilbert goeth to seek a new found land, Sir George Peckham and Sir Thomas Gerrard goeth with him'. This was the first indication that Catholics in England saw a salvation in foreign settlements: 'I have heard it said among the Papists', the spy continued, 'that they hope it will prove the best journey for England that was made these forty years.' The year 1581 had been a hard one for Catholics. The government was afraid of Spanish plots and worried by the influx of priests from the continent. In 1581 the Jesuit, Edmund Campion, was caught and executed. In the same year Parliament enacted severe penalties against the practice of the Catholic faith. To Peckham and Gerrard, both moderate Catholics of means and position, it seemed that a colony allowed them the best way out of the Catholic predicament; abroad they might practise their faith without becoming the enemies of their country. Gilbert, whose greatest need was for money, was prepared to accept finance from any quarter. And any dislike he might have had for his new associates was no doubt cancelled when he learnt that the government approved of the export of Catholics.

One of the earliest arguments for colonization had been that it would rid the state of objectionable minorities, criminals or dissidents. England was now prepared to try this policy; for the knowing ambassador Mendoza reported that it was Walsingham, the queen's Puritan secretary, who encouraged and promoted the Catholic desire to emigrate to a peaceful colony:

Walsingham put it secretly to two spendthrift Catholic gentlemen who have some land that if they helped Humphrey Gilbert in his expedition, they would escape losing life and property, to live in those parts with freedom of conscience and enjoy the use of their property in England.

Since Spain had no wish to see an English colony, Catholic or otherwise, in the Americas, Mendoza was alarmed. He approached the English Catholics and threatened them with excommunication if they set sail, and extinction by the ferocious hand of Pedro de Menendez if they arrived. But it was no part of the English intention to help Spain, and the Catholics went on with their plans.

Gilbert assigned over 8 million acres to the Catholics and their friends; the dashing Sir Philip Sidney received 3 million acres, perhaps to colonize himself out of an ardent desire to see England great, or perhaps to pass on to the Catholics as an intermediary between them and Walsingham, his future father-in-law. At first Gilbert intended to lead a joint expedition, then it was decided that the assignees should make their own way to the promised territories while Gilbert used the funds they had given him for a separate venture. In the second half of 1582 and early in the next year the various preparations went on with many changes of plan, the intervention of new adventurers and the backing out of old partners, with plots and counter-plots, quarrels, mistakes and suspicions. The commerce in the new settlements was given to the 'Merchant Adventurers with Sir Humphrey Gilbert', a joint-stock company based in Southampton. Those who were granted land were to pay Gilbert a small yearly rental, varying between 1s. 3d. and 5s. per thousand acres, and also pay him two-fifths of the value of all gold, silver and jewels discovered in the first seven years. Rights of trade were granted to them so long as they paid Gilbert a customs fee.

Gilbert granted restrictive terms and no doubt asked a good price for his assignments. No wonder many dropped away. To maintain interest in what was an expensive and hazardous voyage with unknown rewards at the end, the adventurers organized a careful propaganda. In the autumn of 1582 Richard Hakluyt brought out his *Divers Voyages*, a collection of documents bearing on colonization, and on the possibility of finding a passage round America to China, which encouraged Englishmen to think the effort both possible and profitable. He gave the example of Cabot whose discovery claimed North America for England; he recalled the successful journey of Verrazano to the middle of the North American seaboard known to the English as 'Norumbega'; and he advocated colonies, reminding his countrymen

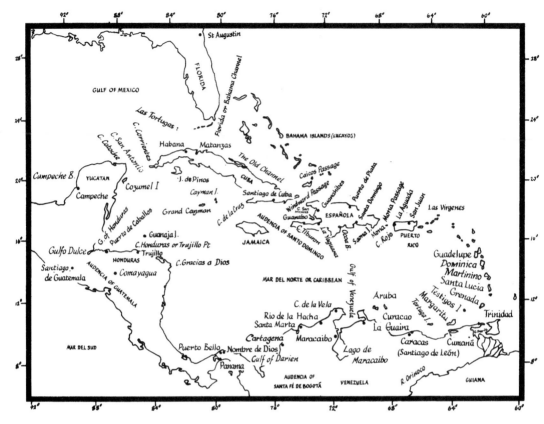

Chart 2   The West Indies in the reign of Elizabeth.

of the happy land settled by Ribault in 1562.

More persuasive arguments were drawn from the examination of various travellers who had been in the New World, particularly from the report of David Ingram. Ingram was one of the men put ashore in Mexico in 1568, after the failure of Drake and Hawkins at San Juan Ulua. He and two companions claimed to have walked from Mexico to Cape Breton before they were rescued by a French fishing boat. The story of this epic feat made strange reading, though some doubted it for 'certain incredibilities'. Ingram confidently anatomized the New World, reporting on its inhabitants, customs, superstition, commerce, cultivation, flora and fauna. He spoke of a town more than half a mile long with 'many streets far broader than any street in London'; he spoke of natives wearing ornaments of gold, silver and pearls, and of houses decorated with crystal and precious metals. He confessed that 'there is great abundance of gold, silver and pearl, and that he hath seen at the heads of divers springs and in small running brooks divers pieces of gold some as big as his finger, others as big as his fist'.

The hope of gain was the magnet for speculators, and Gilbert drew them to his cause by large grants of land and the promise of undiscovered treasure. The virgin land was theirs to ransack as they pleased. But Gilbert himself had a grander vision for his own dominion. On 8th July 1582 he appointed executors for his lands in case of his death, and set out for their benefit his notion of a colony. He saw himself as the sole governor with absolute rights subject only to the fealty he owed to the queen of England. Below him would be a government of counsellors 'chosen by consent of the people'. Landowners were to maintain a house in the chief city, and to keep some of their men trained and equipped for war. The defence of the colony, both by land and sea, would be supported by a levy on all landholdings. Certain lands would be given for the establishment of churches, but both clergy and laymen were to be charged with works for the benefit of the community, with 'the maintenance of maimed soldiers and of learning, lectures, scholars and other good and godly uses in such sort as shall be from time to time thought most meet'. Poor immigrants would be accepted by the colony so long as they brought with them seed and tools to the value of forty-three shillings. Gilbert was jealous of his authority, anxious for his power and profit; but he had a true care for the community unusual among adventurers, and his plan reveals the first practical English colonizer, a man as concerned with planting and building as he was with the accumulation of wealth.

The expedition might have sailed before the end of 1582 but for the constant worry about finance. Preparation was expensive and delay wasted money needlessly. Yet 'bread, beef, fish, beans, pease, bacon meal and such other as was requisite for a long voyage' had to be purchased, and also goods to trade with the Indians. A Mr Ashley of Shropshire, a maker of playing cards, 'had prepared beads and other devices' to venture with Sir Humphrey. Or was the delay rooted in something besides difficulties with money, in Gilbert's factious, uneasy spirit, in his persistent history of failed intentions? Perhaps the cautious queen held him to blame, for at the beginning of 1583 she had Walsingham inform him that he was not to accompany the expedition. He sent back a passionate defence, recalling his service to her, asserting his ability by land and sea, blaming contrary winds for his delay. This venture, he wrote, put his future in hazard, for he had risked all; and he trusted that 'her Majesty with her favour for my 28 years service will allow me to get my living as well as I may honestly (which is every subject's right), and not to constrain me by my idle abode at home to beg my bread with my wife and children'. Her tough heart relented at the thought of her servant's great effort and small achievement, and she gave him permission to go, sending for good measure a token carried by Walter Raleigh, her new favourite and Humphrey's half-brother. 'She wished you', went her gracious message, 'as great good hap and safety to yourself as if herself were there in person.' And she commanded Gilbert to send her a picture of himself before departing.

In mid-March 1583 Mendoza reported that the expedition was ready to sail. But departure was not to be hurried, the formalities of the launching had to fit the grandeur of the enterprise. The learned Stephan Parmenius of Buda was introduced to the venture by Richard Hakluyt and made it his business to commemorate such a worthy project. When Gilbert left Southampton early in June to join his fleet in Devon he was fortified by Parmenius's *Embarkation Ode* of three hundred Latin hexameters. Five ships met in Causand Bay near Plymouth. Gilbert led from the *Delight*, a vessel of 120 tons. His half-brother Walter Raleigh provided the *Bark Raleigh*, at 200 tons the largest of the expedition, though Raleigh himself stayed at home. Third was the *Golden Hind* of 40 tons, once a pirate but now owned by Edward Hayes who was to write the history of the voyage. Next came the *Swallow*, another ex-pirate of 40 tons, captured by Gilbert from the notorious John Callis and pressed into service, pirate crew and all. And last was the tiny *Squirrel*, Gilbert's own ship of many years and already a veteran of the American passage. Hayes wrote of the crew:

> We were in number in all about 260 men, among whom we had of every faculty good choice, as shipwrights, masons, carpenters, smiths, and such like, requisite to such an action: also mineral men and refiners. Besides for solace of our people, and allurement of the savages, we were provided of music in good variety: not omitting the least toys, as morris dancers, hoby horse, and Maylike conceits to delight the savage people, whom we intended to win by all fair means possible.

In this state, provided with help for body and spirit, they departed on 11th June, 'the weather and wind fair and good all day, but a great storm of thunder and wind fell the same night'. Fair prospects declining into darkness.

There was some doubt as to the course. Most were inclined to strike south towards Florida and then to follow the coast north. But the year was far advanced and the fleet was not provisioned for the long passage. Newfoundland was the closest landfall, and there stores could be replenished among the fishing fleets. They chose therefore 'the trade way unto Newfoundland: from whence after our refreshing and reparation of wants, we intended without delay (by God's permission) to proceed into the South, not omitting any river or bay which in all that large tract of land appeared to our view worthy of search'. The journey that began with doubts continued with misfortune, for the chances of the ocean defied even the most careful preparation. Within two days the *Bark Raleigh*, the largest of the fleet, turned back for Plymouth. Hayes thought a contagious sickness drove them back; a sailor from the unlucky ship later claimed a 'want of victuals to perform the voyage'. Gilbert was angry, seeing already the dissipation of his ancient dream, and wrote to his associate Peckham that 'the *Bark Raleigh* ran from me in fair and clear weather, having a large wind. I pray you solicit my brother Raleigh to make them an example of all knaves'. Then came 'much fog and mists in manner palpable, in which we could not keep so well together, but were dissevered, losing the company of the *Swallow* and the *Squirrel* upon the 20th day of July'. At 50 degrees north icebergs passed, vast silent ghosts cruising southwards. The *Delight* and the *Golden Hind* sailed over the shallow fishing banks where the water was stained with 'the offals and garbish of fish thrown out by fishermen' and the air was clamorous with the cry and wails of seabirds.

On 30th July, seven weeks out from England, the coast suddenly rose up out of haze and fog. They were, according to their uncertain judgment, too far north, so 'forsaking this bay and uncomfortable coast (nothing appearing unto us but hideous rocks and mountains, bare of trees, and void of any green herb) we followed the coast to the South, with weather fair and clear'. In Conception Bay they met the *Swallow* again, 'and all her men altered into other apparel'. After the casting of hats into the air at this reunion, Gilbert's joy turned to consternation, for the crew of the *Swallow*, adrift on their own, had recalled the old ways and taken to piracy; meeting a solitary fishing vessel, 'they came aboard the fisherman, whom they rifled of tackle, sails, cables, victuals, and the men of their apparel: not sparing by torture (winding cords about their heads) to draw out else what they thought good'. With the real business of the expedition yet to begin, one ship had fled and another revealed a pirate's colours. The judgment and wisdom of the leader, which relied on such fellows, seemed already at fault.

The fleet swept on, and the same day found the *Squirrel* at anchor, awaiting them at the mouth of St John's harbour. On 3rd August, in confident mood, they prepared to enter even against the opposition of the fishing fleets who knew only too well the danger of unknown adventurers. When Gilbert's patent had been produced to the satisfaction of the English fishermen, his party was welcomed and discovered a small international community. One of the fishing masters (Hayes claimed always an Englishman) was chosen 'admiral' of the port and kept order with the help of his fellow-captains of all nations; the process of the fishing, and works for the repair and support of the boats were well-organized; the men planted simple crops of vegetables when they arrived in May and harvested them before they left in August. Despite this evidence of friendly order, Gilbert decided that his grant allowed him 'to take possession of those lands to the behalf of the crown of England, and the advancement of Christian religion in those Paganish regions'. On Monday, 5th August 1583, he claimed possession of the harbour and two hundred leagues every way, promulgated laws, imposed taxes and demanded the revictualling of his fleet. 'And afterwards', wrote Hayes, noting the formal investiture of England's first American land, 'were erected not far from that place the Arms of England ingraven in lead, and infixed upon a pillar of wood.'

The ships were replenished with wine, marmalade, biscuits, oil; also with salmon, trout, lobster 'and other fresh fish brought daily unto us'. Gilbert sent out his 'mineral man and refiner'--a Saxon named Daniel--to prospect the countryside. Silver ore was found with some excitement. Gilbert was pleased, for his hopes of the New World appeared to be justified; but having only a year in which to plant his settlement and wishing to discover a warmer coast, he decided to press on. For every moment of delay risked a new disaster in his company. Some of his men were plotting, and some were stealing; others were 'sick of fluxes, and many dead'. What with sickness and desertion the four ships were now undermanned; so the *Swallow* was stripped of healthy crew and left at St John's to take the sick back to England. Diminished by one, the expedition sailed from Newfoundland at the end of August as well stocked 'as if we had been in a country or some city populous and plentiful of all things'.

The course was now towards Sable Island in the hope of finding fresh meat, with Gilbert travelling in the little frigate, the *Squirrel*, the better to explore the shallows and nooks of the shore. For eight days they went on, uncertain in their navigation, but passing land where the soil was good and peas grew everywhere. On the evening of 28th August, after further doubts as to the way, they sailed into a calm, temperate sunset to 'the sounding of trumpets, with drums, and fifes'; but the next day the wind rose 'and in the end of their jollity, left with the battle and ringing of doleful knells'. The storm blew south by east, 'bringing withal rain, and thick mist, so that we could not see a cable length before us'. Among sandbanks and shoals the *Delight* struck ground 'and had soon after her stern and hinder parts beaten in pieces'. The two remaining ships, smaller and more manageable, bore desperately to the south, 'even for our lives into the wind's eye'. The *Delight* was lost, and a hundred men with her. Stephan Parmenius, the gallant academic poet so far from his landlocked Hungarian home, perished, and Daniel the Saxon refiner also. Down with the ship, the biggest left to the expedition, went the bulk of the stores: 'This was a heavy and grievous event, to lose at one blow our chief ship freighted with great provision, gathered together with much travel, care, long time, and difficulty.' The calamity condemned the venture to inevitable failure.

The weather continued cold and windy; the winter was coming on and the men's clothing was thin and ragged. The captains were uncertain of their bearings off a coast full of dangers. They called on Sir Humphrey to abandon his search and return to England. Gilbert gave way easily, 'withal protesting himself greatly satisfied with that he had seen, and knew already. Reiterating these words, Be content, we have seen enough and take no care of expense past: I will set you forth royally the next spring, if God send us safe home'. On Saturday, 31st August, in the afternoon, they set course for England and saw at once a walrus swimming by, 'turning his head to and fro, yawning and gaping wide, with ugly demonstration of long teeth, and glaring eyes, and to bid us a farewell (coming right against the *Hind*) he sent forth a horrible voice, roaring or bellowing as doeth a lion'. The men were frightened, but Gilbert welcomed the apparition with a kind of bravado,'rejoicing that he was to war against such an enemy, if it were the devil'.

Their retreat was now as swift as their former advance had been slow. Gilbert varied with the wind, swinging between despondency and exhilaration. The pain of his losses made him beat the cabinboy.

Walruses, drawn by an Eskimo artist. These massive, rugged beasts were new to Englishmen. One sighted by Humphrey Gilbert on leaving Newfoundland in 1583 was taken as an evil omen and a prelude to the disaster that later overtook the little *Squirrel*.

He particularly grieved the loss of his books and his notes, and of something unspoken which Hayes took to be the silver ore that Daniel had found in Newfoundland. Whether it was this foreshadowing of riches or some other secret matter, Gilbert gave up hopes of a southern colony in the warm regions and 'was now become a northern man altogether'. He already had in mind two expeditions for the next spring, south and north, and had no worry for the finances. 'I will bring good tidings unto her Majesty', he told Hayes, 'who will be so gracious to lend me £10,000.' Nothing but the hope of very great treasure could have moved Elizabeth to such generosity, as Sir Humphrey knew well from experience. Between delusion and rapture Gilbert hurried home, refusing to transfer from the little frigate (dangerously encumbered about the decks with too many guns) to the larger *Golden Hind*, saying: 'I will not forsake my little company going homeward, with whom I have passed so many storms and perils.'

Off the Azores they altered course for England to the north and met immediately 'very foul weather, and terrible seas, breaking short and high pyramid-wise'. The seas were as bad as experienced sailors had known, but the worse the storm, the more serene Gilbert became.

From the *Hind*, Edward Hayes observed the mad dance of ship and sea:

> Monday the ninth of September, in the afternoon, the frigate was
> near cast away, oppressed by waves, yet as that time recovered:
> and giving forth signs of joy, the General sitting abaft with a book
> in his hand, cried out unto us in the *Hind* (so oft as we did approach
> within hearing) We are as near to heaven by sea as by land. Re-
> iterating the same speech, well beseeming a soldier, resolute in
> Jesus Christ, as I can testify he was.

The same night, about twelve o'clock, those on the *Hind* saw the lights
of the *Squirrel* disappear. Sir Humphrey and his little ship, for so long
partners in frustrated enterprise, went down together.

Misfortune touched all that Gilbert attempted. Colonization was

Caribou, drawn by an Eskimo artist.

# THE

# PRINCIPAL NAVI-
## GATIONS, VOIAGES,
### TRAFFIQVES AND DISCO-
ueries of the Englifh Nation, made by Sea
or ouer-land , to the remote and fartheft di-
ftant quarters of the Earth, at any time within
the compaffe of thefe 1500. yeeres: Deuided
into three feuerall Volumes, according to the
pofitions of the Regions, whereunto
they were directed.

This firft Volume containing the woorthy Difcoueries,
&c. of the Englifh toward the North and Northeaft by fea,
as of *Lapland,Scrikfinia,Corelia,*the Baie of *S. Nicolas,* the Ifles of *Col-
goiene, Vaigatz,* and *Noua Zembla,* toward the great riuer *Ob,*
with the mighty Empire of *Ruffia,*the *Cafpian* fea,*Geor-
gia, Armenia, Media, Perfia, Boghar* in *Bactria,*
and diuers kingdoms of *Tartaria:*

Together with many notable monuments and teftimo-
nies of the ancient forren trades, and of the warrelike and
other fhipping of this realme of *England*in former ages.

*VVhereunto is annexed alfo a briefe Commentarie of the true*
ftate of *Ifland* , and of the Northren Seas and
lands fituate that way.

*And laftly, the memorable defeate of the Spanifh huge
Armada, Anno 1588.* and the famous victorie
atchieued at the citie of *Cadiz,*1596.
are defcribed.

*By* RICHARD HAKLVYT *Mafter of*
Artes, and fometime Student of Chrift-
Church in Oxford.

*1617*

✤ Imprinted at London by GEORGE
BISHOP, RALPH NEWBERIE
and ROBERT BARKER.
1598.

Title-page to the first volume of the 1598 edition of Hakluyt's
*Principal Navigations*.

his true ideal and he remained, Hayes wrote, 'firm and resolute in a purpose by all pretence honest and godly'. And for seeking to build in an age of robbers, 'his zeal deserveth high commendation'. But nothing grew from his planting; St John's, Newfoundland, waited another thirty years for its first permanent settlers. Though desiring a colony and knowing also, as he showed in his writings, something of the patient effort needed to establish one, Gilbert acted with the familiar bravado of the Elizabethan adventurer, peremptory, rash, lusting after wealth and power, always taking, secretly gloating over his lump of silver ore amid the wreck of his expedition. Hayes, who admired Gilbert a little and criticized him more, taxed him with 'temerity and presumption' for pride and wilfulness and lack of judgment, hazarding lives and livelihoods on an ill-prepared and desperate gamble: 'between extremities, he made a right adventure, putting all to God and good fortune.' Nor was Gilbert the man to undertake the grand enterprise he had conceived. Elizabeth noted that he had 'no good hap at sea'. His knowledge of navigation was theoretical rather than practical, and his impatient, prickly temper fretted in the close confines of a ship. He thrust himself, wrote Hayes, 'into the action, for which he was not fit, presuming the cause pretended in God's behalf, would carry him to the desired end'.

The inconsistency of Gilbert was the mirror of England's uncertainty. No proper provision was made for the work of colonization. The queen and Council allowed settlement as a means to get rid of unwanted citizens, but the burdens of emigration were so great that few could afford them. The Catholics who were to accompany Gilbert were mostly frightened away. Finance was left to the private enterprise of speculators. As the return was unknown and matured very slowly, English expeditions were likely to be always small and under-financed. For the moment, the profits from freebooting were more attractive. But Gilbert's thought at least, if not his practice, was a new encouragement to generous minds. 'We and the French are most infamous for our outrageous, common, and daily piracies,' wrote Hakluyt. Gilbert had asserted, against the opinion of his country, that settlement was a nobler and greater work than piracy, and this became a constant theme of Richard Hakluyt in his *Principal Navigations*, the prose epic of English discovery and expansion.

*6*

# 6

# The Attempt of
# Sir Walter Raleigh

*For conversation of particular greatness and dignity, there is nothing more noble and glorious than to have felt the force of every fortune.*

NO WORLDLY FORTUNE remained from the wreck of the *Squirrel*. In the impoverished estate of the drowned man, ruined by incapacity and idealism, only the colonial dream seemed a worthwhile inheritance. After the winter storms, many preparations were in hand at the start of the next year to complete the work that Gilbert had brought within sight of success. Sir John Gilbert, the head of the family, began plans for an expedition to Newfoundland. In February 1584, Adrian Gilbert, a younger brother, received a patent for the discovery of the north-west passage and from this came eventually the bold voyages of John Davis. Others, besides the Gilbert family, were also active, and the hopes of the Gilberts were nearly anticipated by the energetic interloper Christopher Carlile who, leaving for New England as soon as the skies cleared in 1584, got no further than Ireland. These too-hasty ventures were frustrated by the familiar difficulties of finance and shipping. When the early flurry grew quiet, one man was seen to possess the field. The colonial legacy of the drowned sailor had fallen to his half-brother, Walter Raleigh.

Acting with his usual despatch, and no doubt taking advantage of his position as the queen's favourite, Raleigh was granted a patent on 25th March 1584 to possess all territories newly discovered so long as he did not interfere with the Newfoundland fishing. Raleigh's intention is not recorded. He would aim at a southerly region, avoiding Newfoundland, but whether to set up a base for plunder, a trading post, or a full colony no one knew. Two ships were quickly made ready in the Thames, a pinnace and a larger vessel, perhaps the same *Bark Raleigh*

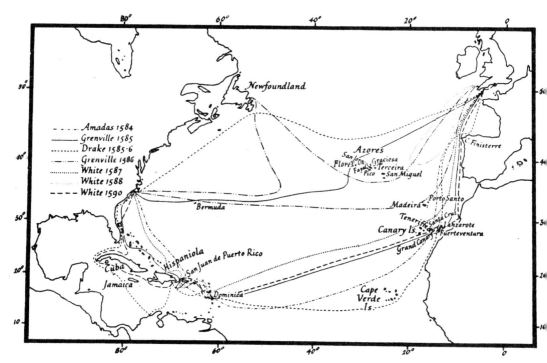

- - - - - Amadas 1584
————— Grenville 1585
·········· Drake 1585-6
— · — · — Grenville 1586
·········· White 1587
————— White 1588
– – – – White 1590

Chart 3   Voyages to Raleigh's Virginia 1584–90.

that had deserted Gilbert's last expedition the year before. From the Thames they went to Raleigh's home country in the West to gather their crews. The captains were Philip Amadas and Arthur Barlow, the pilot was Simon Fernandez, the experienced sea-dog from the Azores who had already served Gilbert. 'The 27th day of April, in the year of our redemption, 1584,' wrote Arthur Barlow in the account of the expedition he later sent to his master Raleigh, 'we departed the west of England, with two barks, well furnished with men and victuals, having received our last, and perfect directions by your letters, confirming the former instructions.' These instructions have disappeared, but the voyage was clearly a reconnaissance for a greater attempt.

A slow but eventful journey. At the Canaries by 10th May, they picked up the north-east trade winds to the Caribbean. Landing in Puerto Rico, they found 'the air very unwholesome, and our men grew for the most part ill disposed', so taking on water and food they departed after twelve days, heading north by the Florida channel. By 2nd July they were in shallow water and smelt the sweet scents of the land. Two days later they saw land then travelled 120 miles looking for a good anchorage on the flat seashore. On 13th July the pilot Fernandez perceived an entrance in the Carolina Banks at Hatarask,

A drawing by John White, engraved by Theodore de Bry. The arrival of the Englishmen in Virginia. 'The sea coasts of Virginia are full of islands, whereby the entrance into the main land is hard to find.' Artist and engraver have garnished the picture with various representations of Indian life, some villages, a fish-weir and dug-out canoes; several kinds of trees are shown, and also a grape-vine. The inclusion of numerous wrecks indicates the difficulties of navigation on the Carolina Banks.

just below Roanoke Island. 'And after thanks given to God for our safe arrival thither, we manned our boats, and went to view the land next adjoining, and to take possession of the same, in the right of the Queen's most excellent Majesty.' Possessors of a new land, they wondered what they had found.

Low sand dunes behind a long line of surf; grapes everywhere in the summer sun, covering the bushes and reaching to the tops of the cedars. Going inland they mounted a rise and surveyed further. They saw they were on a long, narrow island, with open sea to north and south, and the land stretching away to the west. Cedar woods filled the hollows below them, out of which rose, at the crash of a gunshot, an alarmed multitude of cranes. Deer, rabbits, birds of all kinds abounded. The woods contained pines, cypress, sassafras, sweet gum and 'the highest, and reddest cedars of the world'. Sweet and aromatic smells lay in the air. For two days no other human sound broke the quiet rhythm of the surrounding country. On the third day the Englishmen saw a small boat paddling towards the island with three people in it. One of the Indians left his fellows and walked up and down at a point opposite the English ships; as a party rowed out from the ships the Indian waited, 'never making any show of fear or doubt'. Captain Barlow wrote of this encounter:

> And after he had spoken of many things not understood by us we brought him with his own good liking aboard the ships, and gave him a shirt, a hat, and some other things, and made him taste of our wine, and our meat, which he liked very well: and after having viewed both barks, he departed, and went to his own boat again, which he had left in a little cove, or creek adjoining: as soon as he was two bowshots into the water, he fell to fishing, and in less than half an hour, he had laden his boat as deep as it could swim, with which he came again to the point of land, and there he divided his fish into two parts, pointing one part to the ship, and the other to the pinnace: which after he had (as much as he might) requited the former benefits received, he departed out of our sight.

The first meeting with Indians—nothing but courtesy, respect, mutual benefit.

The happy omen of the first contact was the prelude to six good weeks on the Carolina Banks. The Indians were of a Roanoke tribe whose chief was called Wingina. He ruled a village on Roanoke Island and perhaps another on the swampy mainland in a country which the English wrongly thought to be named Wingandacoa. From their round houses behind a palisade of tree trunks the Indians emerged boldly to trade, led by the chief's brother, Granganimeo. They brought deerskins and buffalo hides, maize, fruit and vegetables, and they took away pots and axes and tin dishes. They clambered aboard the British ships in great good humour, tasted the wine and food of the strangers, fingered cloth and sails, touched armour and the bright swords with admiration, and though they offered a large amount of pearls for these weapons the English wisely did not sell.

Daily, gifts of produce arrived at the ships, and the hospitality followed them wherever they went. On a short expedition to Roanoke Island, between the reef and the mainland, a party of Englishmen

A drawing by John White, engraved by Theodore de Bry. 'The town of Pomeiooc and true form of their houses, covered and enclosed some with mats and some with barks of trees. All compassed about with small poles stuck thick together instead of a wall.' This is the earliest and most reliable Western representation of the enclosed Algonkian village. The building marked A is the 'temple' and that marked B is the chief's house.

were greeted by Granganimeo's wife in a typical small village of nine houses, built of cedar and set each side of a broad beaten roadway which led out to the cultivated ground of maize and vegetables. In the best house of the village the clothes of the sailors were taken and washed, and the travellers' feet were bathed; then a feast was set before them of venison and fish cooked in different ways, maize boiled in milk and seasoned, pumpkins, vegetables and fruits of various kinds. No discord marred the meeting of the races.

In six weeks by observation, by signs and mime and guesswork, Arthur Barlow pieced together something of the native life and government. The land was scantily populated with small, independent villages under chiefs who were continuously at war with one another, 'by reason whereof, and of their civil dissensions, which have happened of late years amongst them, the people are marvellously wasted, and in some places, the country left desolate'. The wars, as inconclusive as they were pointless, were treacherously conducted by the men, who wore no armour, but carried clubs, bows and arrows, and a kind of hardwood sword. The inhabitants were attractive, both men and women, of a yellowish colour, with black hair, easy and dignified in their movements. Both sexes wore much the same sort of clothes, a short skirt made of skins and a fur cloak, apart from which the top half of the body was bare. Both sexes wore decoration, painting designs on the forehead, wearing earrings and necklaces of pearls, and copper pendants. The people had a great respect for their chiefs and governors, and worshipped idols. They had little knowledge of metals and no tools of their own, though some of them had taken spikes and nails from European boats wrecked on their dangerous shoreline. The climate was pleasant and the ground fertile. Maize was sown twice a year. Vegetables, fruit, game, fish, timber were all plentiful. Pearls were much in evidence, and hopefully gold and other treasure might be found. 'We found the people', Barlow concluded, 'most gentle, loving, and faithful, void of all guile and treason, and such as lived after the manner of the golden age. The earth bringeth forth all things in abundance, without toil or labour.'

Towards the end of August the two ships left the Carolina Banks, bearing the glad news of a bounteous land and a noble people. Two Indians from Roanoke went with them, named Manteo and Wanchese, accompanying various native wares. With favourable winds the ships were back in the West of England by the middle of September.

Enthusiasm is notoriously blind. Barlow painted a land without shadows, yet he had seen enough to worry a more reflective judgment. Even in clear weather the English had found the long reefs of the shoreline exceptionally tricky. The waters of the sound were shallow; within a hundred miles there was no satisfactory harbour for large ships; the one deep-water inlet, at Albemarle Sound, could not be used, for the reef barred the passage of any ship over twenty tons or so. In fine weather ships could stand off the banks, as Barlow and Amadas had done, but in the season of storms and hurricanes the lack of a decent harbour would work against any settlement, and make the establishment of a raiding base impossible.

Nor was the countryside as welcoming as Barlow thought. The land where it was cleared and firm was certainly fertile, but a very great part of the country was swampland and the Indians were already in possession of the cultivable parts. Were the Europeans to compete with the Indians for this land? Or did they expect to live off the bounty of the inhabitants? The Indians were few in number, simple in their needs; they grew very little more than they could use themselves and it was beyond their capacity to feed a hungry mass of Europeans for any length of time. An unsophisticated people, following the ritual rounds of the seasons, sowing, fighting, harvesting, feasting, knowing little of trade and nothing of manufacture, the Indians could hardly withstand the shock of an ambitious white race, land-hungry, treasure-hungry, contemptuous of all 'heathens'. The power of the Europeans insisted that the original inhabitants should change to accommodate the new ways of the outsiders. Those Indians who could not adapt faced enslavement or extinction.

Arthur Barlow was not the man to reflect on these matters, and nor, at this time, was his master Walter Raleigh. In 1584 he was thirty-two, the rising star of the court, 'a gentleman', as Holinshed said of him, 'from his infancy brought up and trained in martial discipline, both by land and sea, and well inclined to all virtuous and honourable adventures'. By 'virtuous and honourable adventures' the chronicler meant any intrepid and violent act that helped the aims of England. And Raleigh had already begun to prove himself in the service of his country. He had caught the eye of authority by proud, unruly conduct in London for which he had spent a short time in gaol. But Walsingham in particular had noted his spirit and, knowing his parentage and relations, had judged young Raleigh just the man for the Irish wars. In the summer of 1580 he went to Ireland as a captain, to demonstrate once again the implacable, ferocious temper of his family. The destruc-

Sir Walter Raleigh at the time of the Virginia voyages. At this time, in his mid-thirties, he was still the Queen's favourite, a proud and elegant courtier at the height of his wealth and influence.

*National Portrait Gallery*

tion which Humphrey Gilbert had caused fifteen years before was continued by his half-brother Raleigh. At Smerwick, on 10th November, Raleigh's company was one of the two that wiped out the insurgents after they had begged for mercy, slaughtering the Spaniards and hanging the Irish, men and women, almost to the last person. Such butchery, as Gilbert had found, was greeted with favour rather than disgust; Walter Raleigh, without doubt a very stern and resolute soldier, was on the way to advancement.

Effective brutality seemed to give Raleigh a special reputation among the Englishmen in Ireland, and the ambitious young man traded on it. Superior officers, even the Lord Deputy, Lord Grey, who were less eager to kill than the junior captain found themselves boldly reported and criticized to Walsingham in London. Ormond, the commander in Munster was not severe enough, nor was Grey, even though his three-year rule had been an epitome of horror. Raleigh advocated the recall of his bloodthirsty brother Gilbert—what they might have done to the rebels between them! But he could not have his way and grew bored under leaders he thought too tender-hearted. Grey wrote that he liked not 'Captain Raleigh's carriage or company'; in August 1581 Raleigh retorted with contemptuous arrogance: 'I have spent some time here under the deputy, in such place and charge as, were it not that I knew him to be one of yours, I would disdain it as much as to keep sheep.'

He returned from Ireland in December 1581 and soon caught the speculative eye of the queen. Everyone knows the fanciful story of the cloak spread for her over a puddle. Most likely Raleigh owed his good fortune to nothing other than looks and virility. Sir Robert Naunton, who knew him well and helped to send him to the block in the next reign, commented on his 'good presence, in a handsome and well-compacted person; a strong natural wit and a better judgment; with a bold and plausible tongue, whereby he could set out his parts to best advantage'. Elizabeth appreciated young manhood, playing the games of courtly love out of an embittered sexuality, the ageing star to ambitious men twenty years her junior who for all their knowingness could not help but admire 'the wit that turns huge Kingdoms upside down' (the phrase is Raleigh's) in that bony, angular body. Raleigh became her 'Water', a pun on his name and a playful reminder of his foreign ventures. In the spring of 1585 an agent of Mary Stuart speaks of Raleigh as 'the Queen's dear minion, who daily groweth in credit'; two years later another spoilt favourite, Essex, wrote resentfully that 'she came to speak of Raleigh, and it seemed that she could not well endure anything to be spoken against him'. Other sour critics, who wondered that the queen should lavish gifts on this proud, greedy upstart with a broad Devonshire accent, sneered at him as one of her *suavissimos Adonides*.

Picked out from the press of courtiers, Raleigh felt the benefits of royal patronage. Elizabeth rewarded her favourites profusely, but with characteristic shrewdness—not to say meanness—she arranged it so that they prospered at her subjects' expense rather than her own, accumulating confiscated lands, exploiting monopolies, farming the customs. In May 1583 a monopoly for the issue of wine licences put Raleigh on the way to riches. In the next year he was given a licence to export cloth free from the usual restrictions, and thereafter money flowed into his hungry pocket; he farmed out his privileges and collected profitable positions until his income nearly matched his pride.

In 1584 he became a Member of Parliament for Devonshire, like his half-brother before him a defender of the royal prerogative against the hostile men of the Commons. In 1585 he was made Lord Warden of the Stannaries, a lucrative post governing the mines of the West Country. Soon he was knighted, then captain of the Queen's Guard, then lord-lieutenant of Cornwall, and vice-admiral of Devon and Cornwall. In London he lived grandly at Durham House while a confiscated estate provided him with his favourite home at Sherborne in Dorset. He was generally hated. But his desire, as he admitted, was 'to seek new worlds, for gold, for praise, for glory', and this ambition he knew to be expensive. The example of his brother Gilbert, a less worldly man, had shown that sea ventures failed most easily for lack of finance. A colonizer needed money and Sir Walter Raleigh saw to it that he was well provided.

So advancement in England was a necessary prelude to his searching abroad. A homely image expressed the man's incurable itch for knowledge: 'There are stranger things to be seen in the world', Raleigh used to say, 'than are between London and Staines.' Sea water entered his veins at birth; English example and policy added to a restless spirit made the ocean his element. And the extent of his ambition and the height of his vision drove him beyond conventional actions. What were Drake's efforts but glorified piracy? Raleigh scorned 'to run from cape to cape, and from place to place, for the pillage of ordinary prizes'. In 1578, when as a young man in his twenties he had accompanied Gilbert's first expedition, he had (if later accounts are to be believed) run around the West Indies and tilted at Spain. But mature experience taught him that this was a foolish pastime: 'The King of Spain is not so impoverished by taking three or four port towns in America as we suppose.' Sir Humphrey Gilbert had shown the way to a nobler enterprise. Encouraged by the ideals of his half-brother, Raleigh reflected on the near-successful efforts of Ribault and de Laudonnière in Florida twenty years before. Colonization was the worthiest task to be done in the New World; 'this one thing I know,' Hakluyt wrote to Raleigh, whose attempts were promoted by the charitable clergyman with steadfast support and propaganda, 'that you are embarking on the same plan which first the Portuguese, then the Spaniards at length brought to fruition by the devotion of their hearts.' In Florida, Ribault had discovered a land ripe for settlement, and his colony had seemed likely to take root until destroyed by French quarrels and Spanish military power. Now Amadas and Barlow had found a land equal to Florida in every way, or so it seemed from the joyful reports. The time was right for Raleigh to succeed where the Frenchman had failed.

For the moment, his position as the queen's favourite kept Raleigh tied to England. Elizabeth was jealous of her young men and wanted them by her side to flatter and amuse her; it was the price they paid for notable favours. Raleigh himself was prepared, perhaps eager, to travel. He had gone with Gilbert in 1578 and soon after 1580 had taken the Oxford mathematician Thomas Hariot into his household to teach him and his servants (among whom were Amadas and Barlow) astronomy and navigation. But the queen prevented Raleigh from sailing with Gilbert in 1583 and was not likely to release him in the immediate future. He had used his influence at court for the benefit of Humphrey Gilbert, and now that his captains had returned from the American coast with such a favourable report he became the entrepreneur of his own cause, using invaluable connections to set up an expedition that could go without him, and acting with a speed and judiciousness that contrasted starkly with the muddled preparation formerly usual in English expeditions.

New preparations began even before the return of Amadas and Barlow. In the summer of 1584, at Raleigh's request, Richard Hakluyt wrote his *Discourse on Western Planting*, a piece of colonial propaganda aimed at both the queen and the speculators. The return of Raleigh's ships in the autumn, with their cargoes of skins and pearls, with Barlow's rhapsody on an earthly paradise, and specially with the Indians Manteo and Wanchese, was a gift to the publicists, and

Raleigh adroitly kept his project in the news. In December he introduced a bill to Parliament to confirm his title to the discovered lands. He did this so that his plans would become known to the adventurers and the money men, for he did not need Parliament to uphold his rights under a royal patent, and when Parliament tried to qualify his rights the bill was soon withdrawn. And Raleigh knew he had the queen's approval. On 6th January 1585 she knighted him at Greenwich, and soon after permitted him to call his new land 'Virginia' in her honour.* As further marks of faith in him and his enterprise she put her ship the *Tiger* at his disposal and allowed him (it is not known on what terms) some £400 worth of gunpowder from the Tower.

Where the queen led, the private citizen gladly followed. Raleigh quickly attracted the men most likely to advance his plans. The committee in the Commons that considered and reported favourably on his parliamentary bill included the powerful ministers Hatton and Walsingham and such devoted advocates of sea enterprise as Sir Philip Sidney and Sir Francis Drake. With these powerful friends Raleigh could arrange financial support. Elizabeth herself headed the list of backers, adventuring one of her ships and her gunpowder, and the other subscribers stretched from the minister Walsingham to a host of minor gentry in Devon and Cornwall. The resources of the commercial community in London were tapped by the rich merchant William Sanderson who was related to Raleigh by marriage. The loans were to be repaid in the usual way, from the spoils of Spanish ships encountered on the journey to and from Virginia.

The expeditions of Stukeley and Gilbert had been haphazard affairs, relying on luck and chance to see them through. Raleigh's venture was planned with unusual forethought and thoroughness. Hakluyt, in his *Discourse*, had put forward the theory of English colonization based on a most diligent reading of Portuguese, Spanish and French experience. The aims and needs of colonists were minutely detailed and much sound advice was given on who should go as colonists and how they should act. The expedition also had the benefit of some notes on colonial organization and defence, written by an anonymous soldier for Thomas Cavendish. These notes recommended a powerful armed force and

*Raleigh's 'Virginia' lies between Cape Fear and Cape Henry, from 33° 50′ N to 36° 56′ N, chiefly in the modern state of North Carolina but a little in modern Virginia. Exploration inland nowhere extended more than some 100 miles. The Carolina Banks, behind which the colony of Roanoke lay, are now much changed by the action of wind and sea but the details of the old topography may still be seen.

strong forts, not so much from fear of the Indians but to resist the Spaniards. In a practical spirit the notes suggested that a physician, a geographer, a painter, an apothecary and a surgeon should be taken, also 'an alchemist is not impertinent' and a 'perfect lapidary not to be forgotten'; among more ordinary labourers, 'makers of mudwalls' would be useful. As to organization, an authoritarian government was recommended with stern justice and ferocious penalties, not only for acts against the community but also for sins against the Indians.

And Raleigh made preparations according to these thoughtful instructions. John White accompanied the expedition as surveyor and painter, and his drawings of Indian life are an invaluable record of Raleigh's Virginia. Thomas Hariot, the mathematician of the Raleigh household, already had Manteo and Wanchese in his care, teaching them a little English and learning in return a little of their Algonkian language. When the expedition sailed, Hariot went with special instructions to study and record Indian ways and to make certain scientific measurements and observations on climate, geology, flora and fauna. Nor did Raleigh forget the need for military power. Ralph Lane, an experienced soldier of the Irish wars, was withdrawn from Ireland by royal warrant—another instance of the queen's kindness—and assigned to the expedition. The whole venture was to be led by the intrepid Sir Richard Grenville, a West Country adventurer already known for daring enterprise on the seas.

The first months of 1585 went by with preparations well in hand. Though he made his plans with the help of enlightened views, Raleigh would leave nothing to chance and did not neglect the old freebooting ways of gathering an expedition. He had authority to impound ships, men and supplies in the West of England, and at least one of his captains went out looking for prizes. The Dutch later complained that the *Waterhound*, a ship of Brill, was seized and pressed into Raleigh's service, forced to go to Virginia with all its reluctant crew. Another ship, the *Angel Gabriel*, was captured by Raleigh's *Roebuck* and despoiled of goods worth £1,000. The combination of foresight, practicality and ruthlessness was irresistible. By the beginning of April seven ships were ready in Plymouth harbour. This fleet was small for a colonizing venture, having on board only 600 men of whom half were soldiers. But Raleigh intended this party to be soon followed by a larger expedition. The first voyagers were to establish a base on the American coast from which privateers could sally out by sea and explorers by land, the one gathering the riches the other the information by which later

Sir Richard Grenville aged 29. The portrait suggests admirably the
bold, resolute character of the young adventurer.

*National Portrait Gallery*

colonists would live. No colonist sent out by Raleigh could expect a free and independent existence. Raleigh, unlike Gilbert, made no grants of land, nor did he plan a commonwealth of equals. His colonists were the servants of the speculators commanded by a governor of Raleigh's choice. Their expectation was hard work and obedience.

On 9th April 1585, at the 'pleasant prime', the fleet left Plymouth led by Sir Richard Grenville in the *Tiger*, the queen's galleass of 160 tons, with Simon Fernandez once more pilot. Four other ships varied in size from 140 tons to 50 tons, and they were attended by two small pinnaces, all well found, well victualled, under a stern command drawn up as in a military hierarchy. Grenville was the 'general', leader by land and sea, and next to him came Thomas Cavendish of the *Elizabeth* as 'high marshall'; he was assisted by the 'lieutenant' Ralph Lane. Philip Amadas was designated 'admiral of Virginia', second-in-command on the naval side, and under him came Fernandez the pilot. The remaining captains and gentlemen-adventurers formed the advisory council.

Exact plans and intentions ended at the quayside. Once launched, the fleet sailed into a mysterious future, subject to the chances of the ocean and to the whim of men whose greatest principle was their own advantage. Rough weather in the 'Bay of Portingal' scattered the ships and sank the pinnace that accompanied the *Tiger*, but Grenville's boat drove on alone before the fierce winds, sighting Dominica in the West Indies by 7th May. Four days later Grenville brought the *Tiger* into Mosquetal Bay in the island of St John, off Puerto Rico, and sat down there to make good the losses of the storm and to await his other vessels. Elaborate earthwork defences were quickly thrown up under Lane's guidance, a forge was set up and the carpenters got to work on the construction of a new pinnace, fetching timber on low, wheeled trucks from three miles inland under the very eyes of the enemy, 'the Spaniards' (as the journal of the *Tiger* noted) 'not daring to make or offer resistance'. In ten days the pinnace was finished; on 19th May Cavendish arrived in the *Elizabeth* amid much joyful discharge of gunfire.

A forced courtesy prevailed between the Spaniards and their unwelcome visitors, but the smiles hid a keen edge of hatred, and Grenville was glad to go, burning the woods and destroying his camp as soon as the new pinnace was ready. He then sailed into the Mona channel between Puerto Rico and Santo Domingo and gave the Spanish real cause to revile him by capturing two prizes, the first an

Igwano. Some of thes are 3 fote in length. and lyue on land.

John White's drawing of an Iguana. The Iguana, which was new to the Englishmen, was eaten by the Indians and soon esteemed by the settlers as a delicacy.

*British Museum*

empty frigate but the second a large ship of the *flota* laden with cloth and mixed cargo. Lane set off with the smaller prize to gather salt on Puerto Rico and was there surprised by a party of Spaniards. Lane came away safely but he was upset by what he thought an unnecessary hazard of his life for which he blamed Grenville, and the quarrel on this score was the start of the constant bad feeling between the two men: 'it bred', wrote Lane sourly, 'the great unkindness after wards on his part towards me.'

Within six weeks the expedition seemed vastly changed. Seven English ships had set out for Virginia. Here were two of the original vessels, a brand-new pinnace and two ill-assorted prizes scouting the islands of the Spanish West Indies, flouting the old enemy, offering prisoners for ransom, buying pigs, cows, horses, stocking up on salt, sugar cane and citrus fruit, an expansive life of trade and plunder so little harassed by the Spaniards that the expedition artist, John

White, had plenty of leisure to sketch the plants and animals of the Indies. On 6th June, at the invitation of the governor, the English were in Puerto de Plata; having witnessed a bull fight and taken part in a feast, they were selling their stolen goods and buying cattle and harness for Virginia, and hides, tobacco and pearls to gladden the hearts of investors in England.

On 7th June, with holds well stocked and a profit assured, Grenville led his fleet away from the Indies, north-west to the Bahamas, sighting the Florida shore for the first time on the twentieth. The shoals of Cape Fear nearly caught them but next day they were in a safe anchorage (probably Beaufort, North Carolina) and catching great quantities of fish on the tide. Then they went north along the Carolina Banks looking for an opening, and at an inlet called Wococon they prepared to take the fleet through the shallows into harbour. Here luck deserted them: 'All our fleet struck aground,' Lane wrote in a later letter to Walsingham, 'and the *Tiger* lying beating upon the shoal for the space of 2 hours by the dial, we were all in extreme hazard of being castaway.' And the journal of Grenville's ship put the blame squarely on the Portuguese pilot: 'The 29th we weighed anchor to bring the *Tiger* into the harbour, where through the unskilfulness of the Master whose name was Fernandez, the admiral struck on ground, and sunk.' Though the ship, the largest of the fleet, was saved and refloated, the accident was ominous for Grenville's settlers. The ship was so bruised, wrote Holinshed, 'that the saltwater came so abundantly into her, that the most part of his corn, salt, meal, rice, biscuit, and other provisions that he should have left with them that remained behind him in the country was spoiled'.

After the prosperous days in the West Indies, they stood on the sand-bars of the reef, the fleet split, the best ship damaged, the stock ruined, food enough for twenty days only, the party already plagued by dissension and recrimination. In these dark days almost the only hopeful sign was the reunion of the fleet. Of the other boats, lost for more than two months, the *Lion* and the *Dorothy* were discovered by 6th July already on the coast of Virginia, and the *Roebuck* had also appeared by the eleventh. The party was complete but the extra numbers put further strain on the depleted stocks of food.

The time demanded activity and swift decisions, so Grenville drove his men into impetuous motion. Word was sent immediately to the chief Wingina on Roanoke Island and on the sixth John Arundell set out for Roanoke and the mainland with Manteo for guide and interpreter. On the eleventh Grenville took a pinnace, three small boats and a party of some sixty men to explore the waters of Pamlico Sound and the mainland beyond. In a week they visited several villages including a tribal centre at Secoton, saw the large expanse of Lake Mattamuskeet, and followed the shoreline into the estuaries of the Neuse and Pungo Rivers. On the eighteenth they were back in Wococon. In general, the Indians had received them well, though the loss of a silver cup at the village of Aquascogoc drew quick retribution from the fiery Grenville; Amadas was sent back to destroy the village and burn its cornfield.

The English were disheartened by their first exploration, for they could find nowhere suitable for large ships. 'The sea coasts of Virginia', wrote Hariot, 'are full of islands whereby the entrance into the main land is hard to find. For although they be separated with divers and sundry large divisions, which seem to yield convenient entrance, yet to our great peril we proved that they were shallow and full of dangerous flats.' On 21st July the whole fleet sailed cautiously north to the opening in the reef at Hatarask, opposite the south end of Roanoke Island and called Port Ferdinando after the pilot Fernandez. This opening, long since silted up, at least allowed the lighter ships over the bar, though the vessels of deeper draught still anchored out in the roads. Here Granganimeo, the brother of the chief, came with Manteo to the Englishmen and began negotiations for a site. A point to the north of Roanoke Island, near the Indian village, was agreed, stores were unloaded and the foundations of a fort and some huts were soon laid out. Roanoke would do for the present, offering the advantages of its climate, its good soil and friendly Indians. But without a harbour it gave no promise for the future. It was soon decided that Roanoke was at best a temporary refuge. At the beginning of August Amadas went north on a long exploration of Albemarle Sound. On 5th August Arundell left for England in one of the swifter vessels to arrange for more supplies and more armament, and within a week the decision was made for Grenville to lead some of the expedition home also, leaving Lane with a holding party.

In several letters to England, written from Virginia in August and September, Ralph Lane gave the first news from the first English colony in the New World. 'My self have undertaken,' he wrote to Walsingham on 12th August, 'with the favour of God, and in his fear, with a good company more as well of gentlemen as others, to remain here, the return of a new supply.' He faced the future with mixed hope and apprehension, for whereas the land was good and the climate wholesome so that had Virginia 'but horses and kine in some reasonable proportion, no realm in Christendom were comparable to it', yet he was a solitary leader on a difficult coast, surrounded by savages, with 'the charge of wild men of mine own nation, whose unruliness is such as not to give leisure to the governor to be almost at any time from them'. Lane saw the seed of discord and failure in his own party as much as in the strange land.

Grenville in the *Tiger* cleared Port Ferdinando on 25th August, taking with him 'a great amass of good things' to convince Raleigh and the English investors of the goodness of Virgina. Off Bermuda the *Tiger* came up with the *Santa Maria*, a large ship of more than 300 tons straggling behind the Spanish treasure fleet from Santo Domingo. Grenville at once attacked and boarded her, capturing a cargo of sugar, ginger, hides, cochineal and ivory to the value of 120,000 ducats. Transferring to the prize ship, Grenville sailed into Plymouth on 18th October with the glad news of his tremendous profit, and displaying for Raleigh who hurried to meet him not only the goods of the *Santa Maria*, but also the spoils of the West Indies gathered by the *Tiger* on the outward journey. Grenville valued the prize alone at about £15,000 which, he said, would pay a handsome dividend to all investors in the 1585 voyage.

The spoils of privateering had from the first been one aim of Raleigh's venture, and Grenville's piratical energy had made a financial success of the enterprise, relieved Raleigh of a heavy commitment, and pleased the investors. But there were those who thought that a divided interest could do no good to a colonizing venture, and the contrary pulls of spoil and settlement split the expedition. Lane, the settler who stayed behind, accused Grenville of wasting time on piracy in the West Indies, of governing in a tyrannical manner, and of attempting to put Lane on trial for his life. All this was evidence of grumbles and discontent among the English; Grenville had another quarrel with Fernandez, whom he accused of poor seamanship in the grounding of the *Tiger*. These were proud, touchy men, independent and ambitious, many of them more careful of their own fortune than for the well-being of the tender community of colonists. On a far shore, cut off from the ocean by a reef and from the interior by swamp, in a place that was not ideal, with dwindling food for his 107 men (among whom many were the 'wild men' he complained of), Lane had a right to wonder at his future, and to wonder also what help he could expect from the likes of Grenville and Raleigh in England, weighing in their minds the costs of settlement against the happy profits of piracy.

Infant colonies were no stronger than the support they received from the home country. The experienced navigator Michael Lok admonished his countrymen:

> We are chiefly to consider the industry and travails of the Spaniard, their exceeding charge in furnishing so many ships, for this intended expedition, their continual supplies to further their attempts, and their active and undaunted spirits, in executing matters of that quality and difficulty, and lastly their constant resolution of plantation. All which, may be exemplary unto us, to perform the like in our Virginia.

Alas, England did not give the early Virginia this steady support. Lane expected supplies and help by April 1586 and Raleigh, to his credit, made various attempts to meet this obligation. But the state of the time hindered his efforts. The start of a sea war with Spain put new demands on England's sailors. In the summer of 1585 Raleigh commissioned Bernard Drake—a relative of Sir Francis—to lead a relief party to Virginia, but the squadron was diverted to Newfoundland by the queen's orders, to seize the boats and the catch of the Spanish fishing fleet. When the return of Arundell and then Grenville made plain the needs of the Virginia colony, Raleigh immediately began to prepare a ship of 100 tons 'freighted with all manner of things in most plentiful manner, for the supply and relief of his colony'. Troubled times prevented departure until Easter 1586, and the ship did not reach Virginia until 19th June. Grenville was also preparing three ships and many reinforcements for Virginia. He left Bideford on 16th April 1586, but one of his ships grounded on the bar at the mouth of the harbour and the voyage was held up; his little fleet did not arrive at Roanoke until the beginning of August. Both relief parties were too late. Despairing of help, Lane had taken a chance to leave America by other means.

In August 1585, one hundred and seven Englishmen watched Grenville and the *Tiger* stand out from the Virginia shore and rested their safety in the military hands of Ralph Lane. Many campaigns had stamped Lane with the soldierly qualities, and he set out to rule his colony in the only manner he knew how. Vigilance and discipline were his watchwords and he set down, he wrote, 'a discipline which was severely executed, first at sea, and then afterwards by me, in like sort, continued at land'. He had as his chief aide Edward Stafford, a 'gentleman that never spared labour or peril either by land or water, fair weather or foul, to perform any service committed unto him'. For ten months Lane kept a stern course, beleaguered officer in a strange land, watchful behind the ramparts of his well-made fort, suspicious of Indians, turning his hard hand against them to satisfy the needs of apprehensive Englishmen. And in that company, most took a simple comfort in the strength of their leader. In that company of men, fearful of the unknown, only the scientific curiosity of the mathematician Thomas Hariot, and the faithful brush or pen of the artist John White, both sympathetic observers of the Indians, tempered the forgivable insularity of a lonely band.

The fort at Roanoke gave adequate defence and was placed well enough for further exploration but, lacking a harbour, it would not do for a permanent settlement. In the account of his governorship, Lane has little to say on the first months of his rule, but it is certain that he realized the deficiencies of the site at Roanoke and energetically sought more suitable ground. To the south, the English penetrated as far as Secoton, some hundred miles from their base, but were stopped there by difficulties of supply and navigation; 'as for our pinnace, besides that she drew too deep water for that shallow sound, she would not stir for an oar'. With winter approaching Lane decided to leave the discovery of the south to the future. In the north, Amadas, the 'admiral of Virginia', had begun the exploration of Albemarle Sound before Grenville's departure, and this direction seemed more hopeful.

Some time in the autumn of 1585 Lane sent a party a hundred miles north to Chesapeake Bay where they set up camp and wintered among the Algonkians and some of the Iroquois. The Indians were amiable and curious; the land seemed good. 'The territory and soil of the Chesepians', Lane wrote, '(being distant fifteen miles from the shore) was for pleasantness of seat, for temperature of climate, for fertility of soil, and for the commodity of the sea, besides multitude of bears (being an excellent good victual, with great woods of sassafras, and walnut trees) not to be excelled by any other whatsoever.' The indications are that Lane intended to transfer the colony to Chesapeake Bay as soon as relief arrived from England. Chief Menatonon of Chawanoac had told him confidently that if he ascended three days by canoe up the Chowan River, and then marched overland for four days to the north-east, he would come to a country of skins and pearls surrounding a great bay in which stood a well-guarded island set in deep water.

In March 1586 the settlers at Roanoke emerged from winter rest into a native world turned sharply hostile. Lane, the soldier, saw this unfriendliness merely as the kind of irrationality to be expected of Indians. He did not consider what demands his settlers, without crops and with small supplies of food, had made throughout the winter on the meagre stores of the Indians. He thought it sensible to requisition the food he needed from the Roanoke Indians under the threat of gun and pike. Any opposition, even the slightest affront to the English, was met with a great show of force. All this was borne with fortitude and the hope of revenge by the Indians of Roanoke under their chief Pemisapan (formerly called Wingina but having changed name according to some tribal custom). So when Lane took up the exploration of the Roanoke and Chowan Rivers in the spring, the mutterings of Pemisapan went before, forming a confederacy against the interlopers.

Taking his pinnace to the head of Albemarle Sound and then going on by boat, Lane found a meeting of tribes awaiting him on the Chowan River. But war was Lane's element. He attacked boldly and swiftly, dispersed the assembly and took the crippled chief Menatonon as hostage, clapping him in irons and subjecting him to interrogation. The chief was disposed to talk: he told Lane of the inland route to Chesapeake Bay, and promised veins of precious minerals close to an inland sea, at the head of the Roanoke River. Menatonon was ransomed, his son was sent to Roanoke fort for safe-keeping, and Lane set off up the Roanoke with two boats and forty men. But Pemisapan once again anticipated him, warning the tribes on the river that the English meant harm so that the Indians drifted into the woods and left the Englishmen without a chance of getting supplies. Lane went on for as long as his food lasted, then reluctantly turned and came back with the current, fending off Indians, taking fish from the abandoned fish-weirs, and finally killing the English mastiffs and feeding on a porridge of dog and sassafras. By 4th April—Easter Monday—the English party was back in Roanoke fort.

For a while Pemisapan was quiet. In late April a Roanoke elder called Ensenore, who was friendly to the English, died and the chief began a more subtle campaign against the colonists. Knowing the inability of the English to feed themselves, Pemisapan determined to starve them out. Corn had been sown for the settlers which would ripen in July; if the Indians gave them nothing between April and

John White's drawing of Indians fishing. The drawing shows the use of the fish-weir, the dug-out canoe in which a small fire can be lit in a sandbox, fishing spears and nets. A variety of birds and fish are shown, including swans, geese and ducks, skate, sturgeon, trigger-fish, mullet and hammerhead sharks. The laden boat testifies to the good fishing which most observers commented on.

*British Museum*

July, the English would be forced to disperse. Pemisapan abandoned his village on Roanoke and took his tribe and his stores to the mainland where Lane could not easily search him out.

The state was critical: 'If the savages', Lane wrote, 'should not help us with Cassada [Arrow-arum or Golden Club], and Chyna [roots of Woody Smilaxe], and that our weirs should fail us (as often they did) we might very well starve, notwithstanding the growing corn.' To lessen the strain on the supplies of food, Captain Stafford and twenty men were sent to Croatoan, near the modern Cape Hatteras, to fend for themselves among friendly Indians and to keep a watch for the expected relief. Prideaux and eleven men took the pinnace to Port Ferdinando, to wait there for shipping, and every week a party of some sixteen or twenty men left the fort at Roanoke to grub for oysters and edible plants on the mainland shore.

At this time of weakness and division Pemisapan planned an attack, but Lane was not afraid for he had some news of the Indian intentions and he counted one Englishman the match for ten Indians. The hostile tribes planned to congregate for the attack on 10th June, but Lane did not mean to wait. On the last night of May he resolved 'to give them in the island a camisado [night attack]', then to press on impetuously to Pemisapan's village on the mainland. The night attack misfired, the Indians fleeing into the woods with few losses. The next day on the mainland the two sides met in unequal combat, puny bows against guns and armour. Pemisapan, though 'shot thwart the buttocks by mine Irish boy', disappeared into the woods with an Englishman in chase, 'and following him into the woods overtook him, and I in some doubt least we had lost both the king and my man by our own negligence to have been intercepted by the savages, we met him returning out of the woods with Pemisapan's head in his hand'.

The battle was won but the cause of the settlers was still in doubt. The English were split up, in a state of defence, lacking food; the Indians could be counted on for nothing except enmity; the relief ship was two months overdue. A week after the fight word came at last from Stafford at Cape Hatteras, who sent a messenger with news of 'a great fleet of 23 sails', but whether friend or foe he could not say. The next day Stafford himself came in haste. 'He brought me', Lane noted thankfully, 'a letter from the general Sir Francis Drake, with a most bountiful and honourable offer for the supply of our necessities to the performance of the action we were entered into, and that not only of victuals, munition and clothing, but also of barks, pinnaces and boats, they also by him to be victualled, manned, and furnished to my contentation.'

The arrival of Francis Drake in Virginia was not fortuitous, but part of a grand naval strategy directed against the Spanish. In the summer of 1585 Bernard Drake had destroyed the fishing fleet off Newfoundland. The colony at Roanoke (or so it was hoped in England) was even then preparing a base for English privateers in the Americas. And now Francis Drake was on the seas intending some great blow against the Spanish power in the Indies. Drake's brief gave him some freedom of action; no doubt he was expected to use his famous sense of occasion and initiative. His prime purpose was to occupy Cartagena, cross the isthmus and put a garrison in Panama, but he had his eyes open for any other way to wound Spain. He was well informed of the Virginian venture; any help given to the Roanoke settlers was a danger to Spain. Perhaps he had arranged with Grenville to visit Virginia on the return from the Indies; leaving by the Florida Channel he could very easily turn aside to Roanoke.

Twenty-nine ships left Plymouth in September 1585, devastating Spanish possessions from the Galician coast to the American shore. In the West Indies, Santo Domingo and Cartagena were sacked and looted; galley slaves, African slaves and American Indians were gathered together to garrison the Panama isthmus. But at Cartagena sickness among the English soldiers (brought on perhaps by over-crowding among the poor slaves) made Drake abandon the scheme to hold the isthmus, and turn his attention northwards. His fleet watered in Cuba and then, on 13th May 1586, set out for Florida, keeping close to the shore with a view to destroying all Spanish settlements and shipping. At St Augustine, the Spaniards, seeing the formidable size of the English force, prudently slipped away to the interior, leaving Drake to raze the fort and the town, even to the cutting down of the fruit trees. Here Drake took council among his captains, decided to attack Santa Elena further up the coast, 'and from thence to seek out the inhabitation of our English country men in Virginia, distant from thence some six degrees northward'. The decision of the council was the formal acknowledgement of what Drake already intended. His boats were loaded with stores, clothing and equipment for the occupation of the isthmus, and he had gathered a large number of slaves for the same purpose. He meant to give all his surplus equipment and most of his slaves to the colonists of Virginia.

On 8th June, Captain Stafford at Cape Hatteras saw the sails approaching; on the ninth Drake saw the fire-beacon on the sands and sent a skiff for a pilot to take the fleet to Port Ferdinando; on the tenth the fleet arrived, but the larger ships being unable to cross the bar, 'we ankered all without the harbour in a wild road at sea, about two miles from shore'. The next day Lane and Drake met, and the leader of the colonists made his requirements known. He wanted Drake to take away the weak and sick, leaving craftsmen in their stead. He needed 'handweapons, match and lead, tools, apparel, and such like'. He wanted provisions, and last of all he wanted ships and navigators 'not only to carry us into England, when time should be, but also to search the coast for some better harbour if there were any'. With this help the colonists could strike out for Chesapeake Bay to the good land and the deep water they had heard of. Drake met these demands generously. He gave Lane the *Francis*, a bark of 70 tons, with food enough for 100 men for four months, and this despite a shortage of food in Drake's fleet. He gave him also two pinnaces, four small boats and two experienced navigators.

On 13th June, at the very moment when the colony looked forward to a renewed life, a great storm struck and raged for three days. The ships in the roads cut their anchors and ran clear, re-assembling on the sixteenth. But the pinnace and the small boats were wrecked and the *Francis* had blown away. Drake, still anxious to help, now offered the *Bark Bonner*, but she was 170 tons which Lane considered too big for the exploration of the coastline. Alternatively, Drake was ready to take the colonists back to England. Recalling the misery of the present and the uncertainty of the future, and seeing the fleet impatient to leave, Lane's companions saw the hand of God 'stretched out to take us from thence'. Lane agreed and asked Drake to take them all away: 'And so he sending immediately his pinnaces unto our island for the fetching away of few that there were left with out baggage, the weather was so boisterous, and the pinnaces so often on ground, that the most of all we had, with all our cards [maps], books and writings, were by the sailors cast over board, the greatest number of the fleet being much agrieved with their long and dangerous abode in that miserable road.' In confusion and defeat, with the first drawings of White, the notes and specimens of Hariot, even the pearls given by Menatonon, cast into the shallows, and not stopping for three of Lane's men who were away with the Indians, the English abandoned the land which no more than two years before had seemed likely to prove their earthly paradise.

Dejected men eased their rancour with mutual recriminations. Malcontents, or those who had suffered from Lane's discipline, told their stories up and down the country, slandering Lane or blaming Virginia itself for troubles of their own making. Certainly the settlers had the worst luck, from the grounding of the *Tiger* which lost them their provisions to the blowing away of the *Francis* which prevented further exploration. But the chief causes for failure lay with the colonists themselves, and the more sober men among them, such as Thomas Hariot, recognized this. The Englishmen were poorly organized for settlement. The governor, Ralph Lane, was a soldier and he looked on his command as a military expedition; he could plan a campaign, throw up fortifications, fight, but he knew little of civil government and nothing of raising crops and tending animals. Nor was the majority of his company better prepared. Too many were soldiers or adventurers. Hariot wrote:

> Some also were of a nice bringing up, only in cities or towns, or such as never (as I may say) had seen the world before. Because there were not to be found at English cities, nor such fair houses, nor at their own wish any of their old accustomed dainty food, nor any soft beds of down or feathers, the country was to them miserable.

They were mercenaries, expected to labour to bring fortune to investors in England. Their greatest hope was to find treasure and 'after gold and silver was not to be found, as it was by them looked for, had little or no care for any other thing but to pamper their bellies'. They had no curiosity, worked reluctantly, hardly stirred from the fort, despised and bullied the Indians. Lane himself, though a resourceful, accomplished commander, had as little faith as his men in Virginia and its inhabitants. He allowed that the climate was fine and healthy, the soil fertile, but in his view the place had fatal deficiencies: 'For that the discovery of a good mine, by the goodness of God, or a passage to the south sea, or some way to it, and nothing else can bring this country in request to be inhabited by our nation.'

Two men at least, lifting their eyes from the treasure-hunt for long enough to see the land and the people, were pleased with what they saw, recorded it exactly and had a hope for future colonization. The artist John White, salvaging some of his work from the flight, came back with a bundle of delicate drawings of Indians, villages, festivals, customs, of plants, fish, reptiles, insects and birds. At last, and for the first time, England had an accurate and extensive record of how the

Sketch by John White of a
priest. The dress, a short
cloak leaving one arm free,
and the strange shaven
head with the cock's-comb
of hair, were peculiar to the
Algonkian priest.

*British Museum*

New World appeared. And the scientist Thomas Hariot went further
to dispel ignorance and prejudice. Sent out by Raleigh to observe life
and country, he did his task with quiet industry. On his return he put
his observation into a pamphlet that was both a vindication of the
value of Virginia for settlement, and a judicious history of Lane's
colony. His *Briefe and true report of Virginia* was published in 1588.

How Thomas Hariot became wedded to truth, how in a time of
fierce delusion, religious bigotry and blind national passion he
recorded with such persevering sanity, is a part of Elizabethan com-
plexity and a tribute to the new sense of detachment in Renaissance

science. Hariot's purpose was to reassure English gentlemen as to the fitness of Virginia for speculation—'to impart so much unto you', he addressed his readers, 'of the fruits of our labours, as that you may know how injuriously the enterprise is slandered'. To this end he gave a detailed commentary on the natural resources of the land, on the support that the land would give to settlers, on plants and woods of commercial interest, on what minerals may be found, and on what artifacts and commodities would have a value for trade. His reasonable conclusion was that Englishmen could live there easily; all that might be lacking were cattle and domestic animals and certain seeds or plants which could be imported from Europe or the West Indies. And he forsaw, within a very short time, a profitable 'traffic and exchange with our own nation of England'.

To catalogue commodities was a simple matter; it was a harder task to persuade England that the Algonkian people were not the unfathomable, treacherous savages that Lane had painted. Yet when Hariot had finished his description of them in the *Briefe and true report* there were no longer any grounds for thinking them despicable barbarians. His pamphlet was the first, and not the least valuable, contribution to Indian anthropology, having wise and shrewd things to say on language, customs, government, religion and culture. He found the Indians credulous, simple, without science, taking a child-like delight in novelty and toys; but 'considering the want of such means as we have, they seem very ingenious; for although they have no such tools, nor any such crafts, sciences and arts as we; yet in those things they do, they shew excellency of wit'. Their respect for the knowledge and power of the colonists, their wonder at 'burning glasses, wildfire works, guns, books, writing and reading, spring clocks that seem to go of themselves', made them look on the European as perhaps not born of woman.

Hariot recalled awe and curiosity contending on all occasions when Indian met colonist, and the power of the Indians to learn from these meetings is evident. In a year Manteo learnt enough English to become an invaluable guide and interpreter. It was Hariot's opinion that the Indians were well-disposed towards the settlers and did not become hostile until pushed too hard by the English. Even Wingina, also called Pemisapan, the villain of Lane's account, seemed to Hariot a friendly and trusting chief who, out of a natural interest in ceremony, would join the English in prayer. The cause of later enmity, as Hariot suggested in a guarded passage, was English tyranny: 'Some of our company towards the end of the year, shewed themselves too fierce, in slaying some of the people, in some towns, upon causes that on our part, might easily enough have been borne withal.'

The consequence of Lane's high-handed policy was soon apparent. The relief ship arrived in Virginia on the very heels of the departing colonists, searched for the English, found nothing and came away. Shortly after, Grenville landed and made a renewed search, 'himself travelling up into divers places of the country'. He found the huts of the colony forlorn and deserted; the Indians were nowhere to be seen. Determined to keep at least a token possession of Virginia, 'he landed fifteen men in the Island of Roanoke, furnished plentifully with all manner of provisions for two years, and so departed'. Fifteen men were far too few to stand against hostile Indians. A war party landed secretly on the island, seduced the English into a parley, then attacked and drove the English to the sea, burning the camp and killing two of the settlers. The rest tumbled into their boat and put off to Port Ferdinando on the reef. They clung there for a while then wandered on and disappeared, either picked off by the Indians or swallowed by the dangers of sea and land.

Once again so much effort, expense and modest bravery had led to nothing but failure. And Raleigh's land of Virginia was still unproved as a home for colonists. Lane, and no doubt most of his colony, deplored the lack of treasure, and thought it unprofitable for the English until mines were discovered. Hariot asserted the genial nature of the land and thought that a little care would produce valuable commodities. The arguments were balanced.

What now for Sir Walter Raleigh? Two attempted colonies: Lane returned with all his settlers, grumbling of unrewarding days on the Carolina Banks; Grenville on his way back, having left a mere fifteen men to assert the title to Virginia. Expenses were heavy. True, that fierce dog, Grenville, brought in the prizes of piracy, raiding English, Norman and Dutch ships on the way out, and returning to Bideford on 16th December 'laden with sugar, ginger and hides'. But the outlay was very large and not likely to be covered entirely by the gains from privateering: 'recent record shows', Hakluyt wrote in a dedication to Raleigh dated February 1587, 'that you have spent nearly 100,000 ducats [about £30,000] in equipping your new fleets for the establishment of a third colony to open up countries before unknown and inaccessible.' With good reason Raleigh wrote:

My hopes clean out of sight with forced wind
To kingdoms strange, to lands far off address.

But imagination no less than pride demanded a noble commitment. In that same dedication, prefaced to the *Decades* of Peter Martyr, Hakluyt exhorted Raleigh to lead the way to the courts of China, to reveal the mysteries of undiscovered worlds:

> Up then, go on as you have begun, leave to posterity an imperishable monument of your name and fame, such as age will never obliterate. For to posterity no greater glory can be handed down than to conquer the barbarian, to recall the savage and the pagan to civility, to draw the ignorant within the orbit of reason, and to fill with reverence of divinity the godless and the ungodly.

The road to greatness, whatever the cost, was always Raleigh's path.

After the experience of the first settlers Raleigh decided on a new organization and a new plan. Reverting to Gilbert's scheme Raleigh ensured that each colonist had a personal interest in the success of the venture. Each shareholder who would go to Virginia was promised 500 acres of land, and more in addition according to the size of the investment. Wives and children accompanied the men, and the little commonwealth would administer itself under a governor appointed by Raleigh. John White, artist and veteran of three American voyages, was the chosen governor. He was given twelve assistants of whom only the pilot Simon Fernandez knew Virginia. And the new expedition was to head for a new site. All agreed that the lack of a harbour and the dangerous shoreline made Roanoke a poor choice for settlement. Lane had favoured a new attempt in Chesapeake Bay some hundred miles up the coast and Hakluyt, the scholar of the Americas, writing to Raleigh in December 1586, had concurred; 'your best planting', he said, 'will be about the bay of the Chesepians'. White was to call at Roanoke to collect the men Grenville had left, then sail on to Chesapeake for the foundation of 'the City of Raleigh in Virginia', granted a charter on 7th January 1587 and given a coat of arms bearing Raleigh's device of a roebuck—'Viz: On a Field Argent, a plain Cross gules, with a Roebuck proper in the First Quarter'. And with this went the motto *Concordia: parva crescunt*. Colonization was at last planned on a sound basis, no longer an adjunct of piracy but a dignified plantation for the benefit of the colonists who, though they were still answerable to Raleigh, were released from the need to enrich speculators in England.

Three ships cleared Plymouth on 8th May 1587. The governor John White sailed in the *Lion* with Fernandez as master, a fly-boat and a pinnace, both unnamed, accompanied. The colonists numbered 150, men, women and children, though only 108 stayed in Virginia; two Indians, Manteo and Towaye, went with them. White's journal is the only record of the expedition.

Amid the complaints of a weak man the journal records the history of two principles in conflict, the old predatory colonization beloved of Grenville and practised by Lane fighting against the new and more generous scheme which White hoped to bring into effect. The good intentions of White had to battle with the long-established piratical instincts of the navigator Fernandez. The forceful Portuguese pilot was not ready to renounce personal gain, and harried the governor almost with contempt. The bitterness of this humiliation fills the pages of the journal. Following the familiar route to the West Indies Fernandez immediately began to cross the governor. White's first complaint appeared on 16th May: 'Simon Ferdinando, Master of our Admiral, lewdly forsook our fly-boat, leaving her distressed in the Bay of Portingal.' Evidently Fernandez was pressing on in search of prizes with little care for other business. The *Lion* and the pinnace reached the Indies in five weeks and here the disagreement grew sharper. All attempts to collect salt, seeds and specimens of plants for the new colony were (White claimed) frustrated by the malice of Fernandez. And when in early July the company left the West Indies for Virginia, White accused Fernandez of incompetent navigation to add to his other sins; the pilot mistook the coast of Croatoan and then, rounding the modern Cape Lookout in the night, nearly cast away the ship through 'carelessness and ignorance'.

A safe arrival at Port Ferdinando on 22nd July brought no end to the quarrel. White went immediately with forty men to collect Grenville's party before sailing on to Chesapeake Bay. But as the colonists set out in the pinnace, Fernandez ordered his sailors to leave them on Roanoke, allowing only White himself and a couple of others to return; for the summer was far advanced, the Spanish treasure fleet was likely to be on the seas, and Fernandez itched to get among the cumbersome ships of the *flota*. White meekly gave way. Perhaps he was secretly glad, for he knew Roanoke well whereas Chesapeake was entirely strange. They landed on the island as the sun set. No Englishmen appeared; only the bones of one of them whitening on the strand signified that Grenville's men had been there. In the morning the new colonists walked to the north end of Roanoke, where the fort was, and found the fort razed, the earthworks levelled, the poor huts standing in weeds, the ground overgrown with wild melons among which the deer grazed.

Within two days the fly-boat arrived with the rest of the settlers and the whole company began a laborious renewal amid relics of the lost colony. On 28th July the death of George Howe, shot through with sixteen arrows and crushed with war-clubs while out gathering crabs, impressed on the colonists the danger they lived in. The Indians had not forgotten or forgiven Lane's arrogant oppression. Even the friendly Croatoans of the southern sandbanks, whom Captain Stafford visited at the end of July, fled until assured by their kinsman Manteo that the English would not steal their corn. Nervousness induced confusion and errors. A raid against the Roanoke Indians, to avenge the death of Howe, killed a friendly Croatoan by mistake. An uneasy peace was arranged but the spirit of co-operation was long past.

In a month the ships were cleared and ready to sail. The settlement was rebuilt and restocked with the food, stores and artillery meant for the city of Raleigh in Chesapeake. A baptism and a birth marked the beginnings of communal life. On 13th August Manteo was christened and proclaimed, by order of Sir Walter Raleigh, lord of Roanoke and Dasemunkepeuc. On the eighteenth Elenora Dare, wife of the assistant Ananias Dare and daughter of John White, gave birth to a girl who was named Virginia 'because this child was the first Christian born in Virginia'. With the colony established Fernandez was impatient to get away. On 21st August, when the ships were caulked and trimmed and the letters for England were aboard, a tempest from the north-east forced the *Lion* and the fly-boat, lying in the roads outside the reef, to cut their cables and stand out to sea for six days. When Fernandez reappeared (White thought he only came back because many of his crew were ashore) he would hardly stay for a moment. But the colonists, apprehensive for their support in England, had decided to send someone back to guard their interests. Unanimously they chose White himself, reasoning that his daughter and grandchild in Virginia would keep him true to their cause. White gave way after obtaining a certificate explaining to Raleigh why the governor had deserted his colony. There was little time for plans. On 27th August White hurried from Roanoke, understanding that some time in the future his colony 'intended to remove 50 miles further up into the main'. Next morning Fernandez in the *Lion* struck out for the trade routes in search of prizes, and White limped home in the under-manned fly-boat.

One hundred and fourteen colonists—including seventeen women and eleven children—with no help in the present but two friendly Indians and their own inexperience, put their trust for the future in John White's sense of duty. He persevered in his ungrateful task, but to compound the problems faced by this unassertive man the indecipherable current of luck had turned away from the Virginian colony. White was late home, not reaching Southampton until 8th November after a wretched journey in the fly-boat. On the twentieth he reported to Raleigh, who 'forthwith appointed a pinnace to be sent thither with all such necessaries as he understood they stood in need of', and promising 'a good supply of shipping and men' the summer following, led once again by Sir Richard Grenville. The winter came on making ocean voyages hazardous; all naval men were distracted by the growing threat of Spain. On 9th October the government had ordered a stay of all shipping in English ports. The pinnace did not leave. Meanwhile the larger expedition of Grenville was being prepared. By March 1588 seven or eight vessels were ready in Bideford and waiting for the wind. Instead, on 31st March, an order came from the Privy Council commanding Grenville 'upon his allegiance to forbear to go his intended voyage', and to have his ships in readiness for the defence of the realm against Spain. The only concession allowed him was permission to dispose of any ship Drake might not want. At White's earnest entreaty two small pinnaces—the *Brave* of 30 tons and the *Roe* of 25 tons—were allowed to risk the passage at the end of April with supplies and some fifteen settlers.

Sailing in the *Brave*, White took his misfortune with him. The captain was Arthur Facy, a sea-desperado whose only interest was piracy. Once at sea Facy was the enemy of all shipping until he in his turn was attacked by a larger vessel from Rochelle, severely damaged and sent listing back to Bideford with stores gone and passengers wounded. There he was rejoined by the *Roe* which had also abandoned the voyage. To White the calamity was fit retribution, 'God justly punishing our former thievery of our evil disposed mariners'. A determined expedition might still have reached Virginia, but Raleigh and Grenville were both deep in the resistance to Spain and colonies were forgotten. In the summer of 1588 the Armada came at last and was defeated; the autumn saw Raleigh and Grenville in Ireland delivering the final blows of destruction to Spanish hopes.

The year turned with colonies once more in mind. The publication of Hariot's *Briefe and true report* in 1588 restored the good fame of Virginia. White was steadily 'troublesome' on the settlers' behalf. Richard Hakluyt was back from France, in touch with Raleigh and generally anxious to help; his vast and famous compilation, the *Principal Navigations of the English Nation*, was ready for the press. Raleigh's first act was to strengthen the financial support for the settlement, for no doubt White and his partners had found it extremely hard for the association of colonists to bear the expenses by themselves. In March 1589 a further agreement was drawn up joining certain influential and rich men to the association, giving them in return for their investment certain trading rights and tax exemptions in the City of Raleigh. But 1589 went by and, for reasons not explained (perhaps the caution of merchants, perhaps the difficulty of collecting shipping), no expedition set out. For nearly two and a half years the colonists of Virginia had been waiting.

At last new preparations began as an adjunct to yet another privateering venture. Early in 1590 the London merchant John Watts was making ready three ships to go raiding in the Indies. In February fear of another Spanish attack put a temporary stop to all voyages. Hearing this, White approached Raleigh and asked him to obtain the queen's license for the departure of Watts' vessels on condition that they took White and his supplies to Virginia. The license was granted, Watts posted a bond of £5,000 to keep the agreement and the squadron was due to leave the Thames at the end of February accompanied by the *Moonlight*, an 80-ton ship owned by William Sanderson, the business partner of Raleigh, and also fitted out for Virginia. But alas for the probity of pirates. When White arrived with stores and colonists to join the *Hopewell* in the Thames, he was 'denied to have any passengers, or anything else transported in any of the said ships, saving only myself and my chest; no not so much as a boy to attend upon me'. It was the fate of John White to accept meekly the high-handedness of others, and he sailed out alone with Watts' ships, leaving the *Moonlight* far behind.

In the West Indies the *Hopewell* and its two companions, later joined by the *Moonlight* and the *Conclude*, began their freebooting summer, ambushing the Spanish merchantmen amid the islands of the Indies, living dangerously by their wits, taking some prizes losing others, attacking and being attacked. Jamaica, Puerto Rico, Hispaniola,

Cuba saw them pursuing great galleons like hunting dogs, and like dogs also snarling over the division of the prey. By the end of July the *Hopewell* and the *Moonlight* were ready for Virginia and headed north into the season of hurricanes. 'On the first of August', White wrote, 'the wind scanted, and from thence forward we had very foul weather with much rain, thundering, and great spouts.' On the third they were off the Carolina Banks, near Cape Lookout, but tempestuous seas flung them around for a week. A little way from Cape Hatteras they tried the channel through the banks but were puzzled by the soundings; on the fifteenth they anchored in the stormy roads outside Port Ferdinando. A plume of smoke lazed in the air above the isle of Roanoke, 'which smoke put us in good hope that some of the colony were there expecting my return out of England'. After three years Governor White had returned to his charge.

Next morning the guns of the ships sounded off to alert the colonists and two ship's boats set out for the shore. White had with him the two captains, Cocke and Spicer, and a complement of sailors. As they pulled for the land they saw yet more smoke rising from the high dunes to the south-west, so altered course to investigate. The distance was further than they thought. A long walk in the hot sands without water left them parched and exhausted. When they reached the smoke they gazed on smouldering vegetation, lit by sun or Indians, without a sign of man. They retraced weary steps to the ships.

On 17th August, in the late morning of a blustery day, the boats left again for the channel through the reef leading to the island of Roanoke. Captain Cocke, well in advance, got his boat through the breach, but not without danger of sinking, the sea breaking over the boat and drenching stores, food and powder. The wind was north-east blowing directly into the harbour so that 'the sea brake extremely on the bar, and the tide went very forcibly at the entrance'. While Cocke's men dried their things on the shore they watched the other boat come awkwardly at the bar, stagger and overturn. The boat, caught by the sea, was wrenched here and there so that the crew lost their hold and were swept away. Of eleven men, seven were drowned, including Captain Spicer and his mate; and the four who were saved owed their lives to the brave action of Abraham Cocke. After the disappointment of the first day the tragedy of the second so disheartened the sailors that they would only go on after much argument and persuasion from White and Cocke. Delayed by accident and argument they arrived at Roanoke in the dark and were uplifted by a great fire shining through the trees; 'we let fall our grapnel near the shore, and sounded with a trumpet a call, and afterwards many familiar English tunes of songs, and called to them friendly; but we had no answer'. At daybreak they landed hopefully, saw once more burning vegetation, some bare footprints, and then a tree, 'in the very brow thereof were curiously carved these fair Roman letters CRO'.

White took this as a good sign, made according to previous arrangements, that the colony had moved to the friendly Indians of Croatoan —Manteo's people—at the south end of Pamlico Sound. And this move seemed more certain when, coming to the place of the settlement, he found another post engraved with 'Croatoan', without the cross that was the agreed sign of distress. The old settlement was a melancholy sight. Ruined houses lay round a 'high palisado of great trees' in which rusted the debris of the arsenal—cannons, shot, pigs of lead, overgrown with grass and weeds. At the creek, there were no signs of boats, but strewn around were the contents of chests which the colonists had hidden and the Indians had dug up, broken and scattered. There White found three of his own chests; 'many of my things spoiled and broken', he noted, 'and my books torn from the covers, the frames of some of my pictures and maps rotten and spoiled with rain, and my armour almost eaten through with rust'. The settlers driven out, the the arts and sciences of Europe rejected, the land given back to nature.

The hunt was not yet abandoned. As the wind was in the right direction Cocke and White agreed to call at Croatoan. But the weather was so boisterous that an anchor cable broke and the ship seemed likely to go ashore. In the panic to stop it grounding two more anchors were lost before the *Hopewell* made deep water. The winds grew worse, only one anchor of four was left, food was short and a fresh-water cask had been left on shore. Captain Cocke decided to leave the dangerous coast, winter in the West Indies, and return to Croatoan in the spring. The *Moonlight*, undermanned and without master or mate, set sail straight for England while Cocke steered for Trinidad. Once again the unfriendly hand of circumstance undid their good intentions. Such a storm blew up that the *Hopewell* was driven violently off course and sent scudding to the Azores under bare poles. There was no returning now that winter had come; in October the *Hopewell* went on to England. 'On Saturday the 24th', runs the last entry in White's journal, 'we came in safety, God be thanked, to an anchor at Plymouth.' But what of the 114 colonists? No further attempt was made to find or relieve them. Raleigh, even

John White, left them to an unknown mercy, and under this guidance they disappeared. 'And wanting my wishes', White wearily explained to Hakluyt some two years later, 'I leave off from prosecuting that whereunto I would to God my wealth were answerable to my will.'

Money, then, lack of it and desire for more, determined the death of Raleigh's Virginia. On the return of the *Hopewell* it is hard to know what exercised Sir Walter the more—the loss of a colony or the division of the spoils from the summer's privateering. A long wrangle began in the Admiralty Court between the shipowners Watts and Sanderson over the spoils of the *Buen Jesus*, brought from the West Indies by a prize crew. The considerable sum of £5,806 10s. 4d. was at stake and the decision went against Sanderson, owner of the *Moonlight* and Raleigh's partner. For the next season Sir Walter joined forces with the victor and formed a raiding syndicate with Watts. This venture of 1591 brought home prizes worth £31,380 which yielded (after all costs) a profit of £12,500 to be divided among the investors. It was, Raleigh complained to Burghley, 'a small return, we might have gotten more to have sent them a fishing'.

Soon a greater chance came to satisfy the most inordinate money-hunger. Early in 1592 a large preparation was made in which the queen herself ventured some of her ships and in which Raleigh 'laid all I am worth'. Raleigh himself led the expedition until recalled by the solicitude of the queen; he returned to England after devising the plan that trapped the vast carrack *Madre de Dios*, the most valuable prize taken on the seas. But before the riches could be assessed and Raleigh receive his share, he had fallen. He seduced and married Elizabeth Throckmorton. This betrayal of her favour, with one of her ladies-in-waiting, so incensed the ageing queen, at the end of July she sent Sir Walter and his bride to the Tower from where he was released with difficulty. The man who boasted that 'there is none on the face of the earth that I would be fastened unto' now indeed walked alone until his perplexed dreams led him the way to the headsman's block.

The timid retreat of idealism before the wanton charms of money did not afflict Raleigh alone. His philanthropy, slight thing that it was, had always been governed by the tight reins of his selfishness. All his ventures were business ventures, and colonization differed from the rest only in visionary and imaginative scope. Others, too, began to feel that their initial hopes for Virginia were too sanguine. Those simple, ingenuous seamen Amadas and Barlow had taken a low swamp behind a dangerous reef for the promised land. The light of reality revealed (or so it seemed to many disappointed men) a country with more deficiencies than good points. A sailor who visited the American shore with Drake in 1587 compared Virginia unfavourably with Florida: the more northerly coast was 'indifferently fruitful' and only good for fish, land turtles, nice fruits and saxifrage. The Indians, who at first had the appeal of friendly innocents, appeared in time wretched, dissimulating savages. Even Hakluyt lost faith in Indian nobility. Writing also in 1587 he approved firm action against 'such stubborn savages as shall refuse obedience to her Majesty'. The unvoiced conclusion of England in 1590 agreed with Ralph Lane, that colonization in Virginia was disagreeable and unprofitable; unless mines were found, or a way through to more attractive lands, a settlement was more troublesome and expensive than it was worth.

7

# 7
# Conclusion

*History an interminable and perplexed dream; a dream of recurring forms.*

GOOD HOPES decayed in so short a time. In 1586 the Spanish counsellors of Philip II were railing against 'the barbarous foreigners who spread themselves over the earth in search of rich and fertile lands were they can settle. It is greatly to be feared that so long as the Queen is alive they may extend still further the plundering of the Indies'. By 1590 those fears were eased; the Virginia colony—so threatening to the Spanish, so hopeful for the English—was lost. No successful colonies were planted in Elizabeth's long reign. The attempt of Stukeley was a false start, an intemperate jest. Gilbert gave a promise of success. Raleigh, in six years of fitful care, brought matters to a culmination and a death. But the failure to take root was not for lack of energy. For bold men, confident of their power and curious to extend their ambition, the mere existence of America drew them to it. 'Even if the breath of hope which blows on us from that New Continent were fainter than it is and harder to perceive,' wrote Francis Bacon in the voice of the age, 'yet the trial must by all means be made.' The fault was in the men and the times. 'I am sometimes troubled', Montaigne wrote as he viewed the European descent on the Indians, 'that we were not sooner acquainted with these people, and that they were not discovered in those better times when there were men much more able to judge of them than we are.'

After failure came the analysis of the reasons for an untimely demise. Some things were easy to say: rashness, greed, haste were all too much in evidence. 'Planting of countries', the judicial tones of Bacon lectured in his essay *Of Plantations*, 'is like planting of woods; for you must take account to lose almost twenty years' profit, and expect your recompense in the end.' The experience of a practical navigator echoed the opinion of the philosopher. Why did we not take the example of Spain, wrote Michael Lok, and support Virginia with patient persistence? 'For although it yield not gold, yet it is a fruitful, pleasant country, replenished with all good things necessary for the life of man, if they be industrious, who inhabit it.'

In the clipped epigrams of his worldly wisdom Bacon set out the true ideal of settlement, from which the English colonizers had so woefully lapsed. Choose your land well and plant 'in a pure soil'. Choose your colonists even more carefully, taking not so many soldiers and drones of the community, but 'gardeners, ploughmen, labourers, smiths, carpenters, joiners, fishermen, fowlers, with some few apothecaries, surgeons, cooks, and bakers'. Beware especially of taking criminals and unwanted men:

> It is a shameful and unblessed thing to take the scum of people and wicked condemned men to be the people with whom you plant; and not only so, but it spoileth the plantation; for they will ever live like rogues, and not fall to work, but be lazy, and do mischief, and spend victuals, and be quickly weary, and then certify over to their country to the discredit of the plantation.

Take stock and seed with you, those that will adapt to a new country quickest and with the least labour: 'For wheat, barley, and oats, they ask too much labour; but with pease and beans you may begin, both because they ask less labour, and because they serve for meat as well as for bread.' Let the government of the colony rest on one outstanding man aided by a council, 'and let those be rather noblemen or gentlemen than merchants; for they look ever to the present gain'. Send supplies regularly, avoid marshy and unhealthy ground, deal well and justly with the Indians. 'If you plant where savages are, do not only entertain them with trifles and gingles, but use them justly and graciously, with sufficient guard nevertheless.' Protect them, but keep out of their wars; send some to England so that, on their return, they become advocates of the wonders they have seen. Do all this and a colony will grow. Neglect it and a colony will die, which in itself is a great crime. 'It is', Bacon severely concluded, 'the sinfullest thing in the world to forsake or destitute a plantation once in forwardness; for, besides the dishonour, it is the guiltiness of blood of many commiserable persons.' By this judgment, from the keenest intellect of the age, the colonizers of Tudor England stand condemned.

Reflection is partial. Lordly, unhurried opinion forgets the struggles and perplexity of the moment. All the mistakes were made, but by the best advice. Were soldiers not the men for colonies? Did military training partly prevent the success of Stukeley, Gilbert, Raleigh, Lane, Grenville? Yet Bacon himself insisted that only a nation of warlike men could extend its dominion. 'Above all,' he wrote in his *True Greatness of Kingdoms*, 'for empire and greatness it importeth most that a nation do profess arms as their principal honour, study, and occupation.' Are merchants to be distrusted? Did the pressure of speculators, of great merchants like Watts and Sanderson, squeeze the colony? Merchants, wrote Bacon, 'are *vena porta*; and if they flourish not, a kingdom may have good limbs, but will have empty veins, and nourish little.' Are unwanted men the bane of colonies? Did the indolent hirelings on Lane's expedition waste the resources of Virginia? But the New World, Richard Hakluyt wrote, was the very place for excess population:

> Seeing therefore we are so far from want of people, that retiring daily home out of the Low Countries they go idle up and down in swarms for lack of honest intertainment, I see no fitter place to employ some part of the better sort of them trained up thus long in service, than in the inwards parts of the firm of Virginia.

And lastly, was an incontinent desire for treasure the fatal weakness of English colonization? No nation, Bacon insisted, could expand and become great without great wealth. 'For money,' he wrote in *Considerations touching a War with Spain*, 'no doubt it is the principal part of the greatness of Spain.'

A reconciliation of impossible opposites. It was the unreflective conceit of the colonizers that they could do it all: plant a settlement, bring down the Spanish empire, foster exploration and science, instil civilization and true religion, open new commerce, and gain for themselves unimaginable wealth. The clangorous trumpets of riches, the drums of nationalism beat in their veins. The promise of gold, like a cyclic whisper, rebounds from man to man. The constant hope of explorers and colonizers was the transmutation of base lands into precious metals.

Spain had found gold and Spain became great. 'By the abundant treasure of that country', said Raleigh, 'the Spanish king vexeth all the princes of Europe, and is become in a few years from a poor king of Castile the greatest monarch of this part of the world.' If it were riches that kept England from a similar destiny, then it became a noble, patriotic task to pursue wealth by all means. But Spain had possessed a strong, well-tried army; the *conquistadores* were state officers, supported by the home government with men and transport and supplies. England had no comparable army, and for reasons of expense and suspicion was unwilling to raise one. The work of expansion, which Spain had done through powerful and well-supported generals, in England was left to the private enterprise and initiative of certain sea adventurers, for whom patriotism was its own reward, and who could look to their government for little more than connivance and a small investment. Sir Francis Drake and Sir Walter Raleigh, two who did more than most to make the world fear a resurgent England, both died disgraced. Both tried to redeem themselves by demonstrating their old qualities to a callous government. Both failed. Drake died in the West Indies, sick and sick at heart, dwelling on past glory and puzzled by the alteration in the world he had once dominated, complaining pathetically to Thomas Maynard 'that he was as ignorant of the Indies as myself, and that he never thought any place could be so changed, as it were from a delicious and pleasant arbour into a waste and desert wilderness'. Raleigh pledged a ruined name on the discovery of El Dorado, and when he returned from Guiana without the riches that alone would placate the government, found his reward in prison where he had, instead of action, the consolation of history (of memory) till eventually led out to the executioner's block.

'God hath many things in store for us,' said Drake with desperate confidence amid the shambles of his last journey; 'and I know many ways to do her Majesty good service, and to make us rich.' What delusion kept such men true to that ghostly, unwarranted ideal? The country they served was a cruel deity, demanding limitless offerings of success. Maynard commented on Drake in his final days,

> It fared with him as with some careless living man who prodigally consumes his time, fondly persuading himself that the nurse that fed him in his childhood will likewise nourish him in his old age, and, finding the dug dried and withered, enforced then to behold his folly, tormented in mind, dieth with a starved body.

Enforced to behold his folly, tormented in mind: surely the melancholy and predestined expectation of the Elizabethan adventurer. Raleigh spoke of 'those inmost and soul-piercing wounds which are ever aching while uncured'. The body expended itself in animal vigour on obscure ventures with a kind of overwhelming ferocity, repeated and obstinate acts of grandeur, the wild outflinging of passionate men. Grenville, said the Dutchman Linschoten, 'was of so hard a complexion, that as he continued among the Spanish captains, while they were at dinner or supper with him, he would carouse three or four glasses of wine, and in a bravery take the glasses between his teeth and crash them in pieces and swallow them down, so that oftentimes the blood ran out of his mouth.' Their deeds were the bravado of an egotism that was sometimes noble and generous, but always limited, careless of the future, self-seeking. After a while, when the country discarded them, memory already began to deny them the fame of settled achievement. Nothing remained but the faint din of distant action.

After the energy of the body came the despair of the mind. The days wound down towards an evening, 'and the world's tragedy and time', wrote Raleigh, 'are near at an end'. No work of man could defy the crude annihilation of time, and in this conviction lay the failure of all their colonial attempts. Neither defeat nor victory was important. The only consolation and greatness were in action, and some defeats were worth many victories: Stukeley on the stony ground, dead among kings; Gilbert book in hand on the violent deck, at his ease amid the final tempest; Grenville and his shot-through *Revenge*, dragging a part of the Spanish navy into the Atlantic depths; Raleigh returning peacefully from Guiana to certain prison and at last his death.

# Index

*(Entries in italics refer to captions)*

Africa, 14, 21, 48
Albemarle Sound, 141, 152, 155, 156
Alcazar, 69, 89
Alexander VI, Pope, 98
Alexandria, 25
Aleyn, Charles, 21
Amadas, Philip, 136, 141, 145, 149, 152, 155, 172
America, 14, 27, 49, *54*, *56*, 57, 64, 65, 75, 110, 119, 121, 126, 173, 177; Central, 18, 74; South, 18, 31, 64
Ango, Jean, 74
Anticosti, 113
Antillia, 14
Aristotle, 11
Artois, 71
Arundell, John, 151, 152, 154
Ashley, Katherine, 99
Asia, 14, 18, 24, 27, 49
Asshehurst, Thomas, 28
Athens, 11
Atlantic Ocean, 11, 14, *15*, 20, *22*, *26*, 116
Atlantis, 12
Avon Gorge, *29*
Ayala, 25
Azores, 14, 20, *26*, 27, 128

Bacon, Francis, 37, 46, 177, 178, 179
Bahamas, 17, 151
Barcelona, 18
Barlow, Arthur, 136, 138, 140, 141, 145, 172
Bermuda, 153
Borough, Stephen, 33, 55, 101
Brasil, 14, 20, 21, 22
Brazil, 24, 44, 46, 74, 99, 117
Bruegel, Peter, *38*, *39*, *40*
Bristol, *19*, 20ff., *30*, 42
Burghley, 172
Butts, Thomas, 45

Cabot, John, *17*, 18, 19ff., *22*, 47, 48, 61, 64, 75, 121; Sebastian, 31, *32*, 48, 49, 54, 61, 64, 75, 103
Calais, 42, *43*
Callis, John, 115, 124
Camden, William, 90
Campion, Edmund, 120
Canada, 117
Canary Islands, 14, 136
Cantino, *22*
Cape Breton, 45, 122
Cape Fear, 151
Cape Hatteras, 158, 159, 170
Cape Lookout, 166, 170
Cape Race, 23
Cape St Vincent, 46
Carew, Sir George, 41; Sir Peter, 88
Caribbean, 45, 74, 112, 136
Carlile, Christopher, 59, 135
Carolina Banks, 136, *137*, 138, 140, 151, 164, 170
Cartagena, 159
Cartier, Jacques, 99, 119
Cathay, 13f., 21, 119
Cavendish, Thomas, 146, 149
Cecil, William, 82, 88, 89, 90, 91, 104, 107
Chancellor, 48, 55, 101
Chapuys, 44
Charles, Emperor, 71, 91
Charles VIII of France, 16
Charlesfort, 75, 85, 89, 97, 98
Chesapeake Bay, 155, 156, 160, 165, 166, 167
China, 13, 48, 165
Chowan River, 155, 156
Churchyard, Thomas, 105, 112, 115
Cibola, 78
Cinque Ports, 44
Cipangu, 13f., 21, 22, 25
Cobham, 88, 89

Cocke, Abraham, 170, 171
Columbus, Bartholomew, 16, 21, 46; Christopher, 11, 14, 15ff., *17*, 20, 21, 24, 25, 48
Conception Bay, 125
Constantinople, 14
Contarini, *54*
Cornwall, 72, 116, 144
Corte Real brothers, *26*, 27, *54*
Cortes, 48
Cosmas, 12
Cotswolds, 20
Courtenay, 88
Croatoan, 166, 171
Cuba, 17, 18, 113, 117, 159, 170
Curtis, Ann, 71; Sir Thomas, 72
Custodis, Hieronimo, *109*

Da Gama, Vasco, 27
D'Ailly, Pierre, 15
Dare, Ananias, 167; Elenora, 167
Dartmouth, *86*, 101, 115, 116, 120
Davis, John, 59, 135
Day, John, 21, 24
De Bry, Theodore, *137*, *139*
De Coligny, Gaspard, 74
Dee, Dr John, 110, 119
De la Cosa, Juan, *17*
De la Pierria, Albert, 83f.
De Laudonnière, René, 75, 76, 84, 97, 145
De Menendez, Pedro, 98, 99, 121
Denmark, 48
Denye, Edward, 115
De Quadra, Alvarez, 79, 90
De Silva, Guzman, 85
De Triana, Rodrigo, 16
Devon, 69, 72, 144
Dominica, 149
Dorset, 144
Drake, Bernard, 154, 159; Sir Francis, 46, 61, 74, 91, 112, 117, 122, 144, 146, 158, 159, 160, 168, 173, 180
Dublin, 88, 107
Dudley, Lord Robert, 72, 73
Dursey Head, 23

Eden, Richard, 48, 54, 56, 64, 99, 119
Edward VI, King, 90
Elizabeth I, Queen, 46, 47, 48, 56, 58, 61, 72, 73, 75, 79, 82, 88, 89, 90, 91, 93, 99, 101, 105, 107, 108, 112, 113,

115, 131, 143, 145, 172, 177
Elliot, Hugh, 20
Encisco, 119
Ensenore, 156
Eratosthenes, 11
Erikson, Leif, 14
Erne River, 106
Escalante, 119
Eskimos, 28, *118*, *128*, *129*
Essex, Earl of, 143
Exeter, *86*

Facy, Arthur, 168
Ferdinand and Isabella of Spain, 16, 18
Fernandes, Francisco, 28; João, *26*, 27, 28
Fernandez, Simon, 114, 115, 119, 136, 149, 151, 152, 153, 165, 166, 167, 168
FitzMaurice, James, 105, 108, 116
Fletcher, Francis, 61
Fleury, Jean, 74
Floating Islands, 12
Florida, 55, 64, 73, 74f., 85, 88, 89, 90, 97, 98, 99, 101, 114, 117, 125, 136, 145, 151, 159, 172
Fort Coligny, 74
Fortunate Isles, 11
Frampton, John, 119
France, 21, 37, 47, 48, 56, 70, 74, 75, 76, 82, 97, 101, 113, 146
Frobisher, Martin, *56*, 88, *111*, 112, 117, *118*, 119
Fuller, Thomas, 48, 92

Ganges River, 18
Gascoigne, George, 111, 112
Genoa, 12
Gerrard, Sir Thomas, 120
Gilbert, Adrian, 135; Sir Humphrey, 33, 55, 56, 59, 62, 63, 64, 65, 97–131 *passim*, *100*, *103*, *106*, *128*, 135, 136, 143, 144, 145, 149, 165, 177, 179, 181; Sir John, 135
Gomara, 119
Gonsalves, João, 28
Granganimeo, 138, 140, 152
Gravesend, 33, 79
Greece, 11
Greenland, 14, 27, 28
Grenville, Sir Richard, 91, 107, 147ff., *148*, 159, 164, 166, 168, 179, 181
Grey, Lord, 143

Guevara, 119
Guernache, 84
Guiana, 180, 181
Guinea, 44

Hakluyt, Richard, 33, 45, 46, 47, *56*,
  57, 58, 59, *60*, 62, 63, 64, 65, 76,
  *130*, 131, 145, 146, 164, 165, 169,
  172, 173, 179; the Elder, 113, 114,
  119, 121, 124
Hariot, Thomas, 145, 147, 152, 155,
  160, 161, 162, 163, 164, 169
Hatton, 146
Hawkins, John, 46, 97, *109*, 110, 117,
  122; William, 44, 46, 82, 89, 91
Hayes, Edward, 116, 117, 124, 125, 126,
  128, 129, 131
Henry II of France, 91
Henry VII, King, 16, 21, 22, 23, 24, 25,
  27, 28, 31, 37, 46, 47, 61
Henry VIII, King, 33, 37f., 44, 47, 48,
  53, *56*, 63, 64, 69, 99
Herrera, 45
Heywood, Thomas, 92
Hispaniola, 169
Hoefnagle, *19*
Holinshed, 141, 151
Hooker, John, 101
Hore, Master, 44
Howe, George, 167
Hudson Bay, 31; River, 114

Iceland, 14, 20, 24, 44
India, 11, 27
Indian Ocean, 21
Indians, American, 58, 62, 75f., 83, 84,
  97, 120, *137*, 138f., *139*, 145, 146, 147,
  152, 155f., *157*, 158, 161, *162*, 163,
  164, 167, 171, 173, 177, 178
Indochina, 18
Ingram, David, 122
Ireland, 20, 23, 48, 55, 82, 88, 89, 104ff.,
  *106*, 116, 117, 135, 141, 143, 168

Jamaica, 169
Japan, 48, *54*, 101, *103*
Jason, 11
Jenkinson, 101, 102, 104

Ketel, Cornelius, 111
Khan, Great, 13, 24, 44, 45
Knollys, Henry, 115, 116, 117; Sir

Francis, 107

Labrador, *22*, 30
La Chère, 84, 85
Lake Mattamuskeet, 152
Lane, Ralph, 147, 149ff., 166, 173, 179
Las Casas, 20
Le Havre, 99, 101
Lincoln, Lord, 115
Linschoten, 181
Lloyd, John, 20
Lok, Michael, *56*, 112, 154, 178
London, 24, 25, 42, 72, *80*, 144, 146

Madoc, Prince, 57
Madrid, 88, 89
Magellan, 48
Maguire, Hugh, *106*
Mandeville, Sir John, 12, 13
Manoel, King, 27
Manteo, 140, 145, 147, 151, 152, 163,
  166, 167, 171
Mary, Queen (Stuart), 143
Mary, Queen (Tudor), 55, 71, 72
Maynard, Thomas, 180
Mecca, 19
Mediterranean, 44
Menatonon, Chief, 155, 156, 160
Mendoza, 114, 116, 117, 120, 121, 124
Mexico, 14, 78, 122; Gulf of, 98
Middle East, 101
Milan, Duke of, 24
Millerd, James, 29, *30*
Montaigne, 177
Moors, 16
More, Thomas, 33
Morgan, Miles, 116
Morocco, 69
Muscovy Company, 101, 102, 103, 105,
  107, 112

Naunton, Sir Robert, 143
Netherlands, 74, 110; Spanish, 71
Neuse River, 152
New England, 135
Newfoundland, 20f., *22*, 30, 44, 45, 64
  113, 125f., *128*, 135, 154, 159
Norsemen, 14
North Carolina, 151
North Sea, 44
Northumberland, 70
Norway, 20

Nova Scotia, 30

O'Neill, Shane, 73, 104
Ophir, 12
Ormond, 143
Ottoman Turks, 13
Oviedo, 45
Oxenham, John, 112

Palos, 16
Pamlico Sound, 152
Panama, 112, 159
Parmenius, Stephan, 124, 127
Pasqualino, Lorenzo, 24, 25
Peckham, Sir George, 57, 58, 62, 63, 65,
    120, 125
Pelham, Sir William, 57
Peminapan, Chief, *see* Wingina
Perrot, Sir John, 108
Persia, 101
Peru, 112, 119
Philip II of Spain, 91, 177
Picardy, 71
Pius Quintus, Pope, 92
Pizarro, 48
Plymouth, 44, 82, 110, 124, 125, 147,
    149, 153, 159, 166, 171
Pollard, 88
Polo, Marco, 13f., 21, 26, 62
Port Ferdinando, 152, 153, 158, 160,
    164, 170
Port Royal (Fla), 55, 75, 83, 89, 97, 98
Portsmouth, 37
Portugal, 14, 15, 16, 21, 22, 26, 27, 54,
    57, 58, 64, 74, 89, 102, 113, 146
Prester John, 12
Prideaux, 158
Puebla, 22, 23, 46
Puerto de Plata, 151
Puerto Rico, 44, 45, 136, 149, 150, 169
Pungo River, 152

Raleigh (city), 167, 169
Raleigh, Sir Walter, 46, 55, 74, 91, 99,
    108, 110, 116, 124, 135-173 *passim*,
    *136, 142*, 177, 179, 180, 181
Rastell, John, 33, 53
Reneger, Robert, 46, 47
Ribault, Jean, 55, 73f., 84, 90, 97, 98,
    99, 117, 122, 145
Rio de Janeiro, 74
Roanoke Island, 137, 138, 151, 152, 154,

155, 156, 158, 159, 164, 165, 166,
    167, 170; River, 156
Roberval, 99
Rome, 92
Russia, 48, 101, 102
Rut, John, 44, 45

Sable Island, 126
St Augustine, 98, 159
St Brendan, 11
St John (island), 149
St John (Nfld), 23, 126
St Lawrence River, 99
St Leger, 107
St Mark, 23
Sanderson, William, 146, 169, 172, 179
San Juan Ulna, 122
San Salvador, 17
Santa Elena, 159
Santo Domingo, 45, 113, 119, 149, 153,
    159
Savoy, Duke of, 91
Scotland, 48, 70
Sebastian of Portugal, 89
Secoton, 155
Seneca, 11
Seven Cities, 14, 24
Seville, 20
Sidney, Sir Henry, 104, 105, 107; Sir
    Philip, 121, 146
Smerwick, 143
Somerset, 44
Soncino, 24
Soranzo, 44
Southampton, 121, 124, 168
Spain, 16, 19, 21, 22, 22, 23, 25, 31, 33,
    37, 45, 48, 53, 56, 57, 58, 62, 63, 64,
    72, 74, 83, 98, 102, 112, 113, 121, 145,
    146, 149, 154, 159, 168, 177, 178, 179,
    180
Spanish Main, 74
Spice Islands, 101, 119
Spicer, Captain, 170
Stafford, Edward, 154, 158, 159, 167
Stow, John, 48
Strabo, 11
Stukeley, Thomas, 69-93 *passim, 70*, 99,
    101, 146, 177, 179, 181
Suffolk, Duke of, 69, 70
Sussex, *47*; Lord, 88

Tartary, 20

Thevet, André, 99
Thomas, John, 28
Thorne, Robert, 20, 22, 53, 56, 63, 64
Throckmorton, Elizabeth, 172
Thule, 11
Tordesillas, Treaty of, 22, 23
Toscanelli, Paolo, 15
Towaye, 166
Trinidad, 171
Tuscany, 12

Valencia, 18
Van den Wyngaerde, Anthony, 80
Venezuela, 17
Venice, 12, 18, 23, 33
Vergil, Polydor, 25
Verrazano, 56, 121
Vespucci, 48
Vienna, 14
Villegagnon, 74, 99
Vinland, 14
Virginia, 136, 137ff., 137, 142, 146 and
n, 147ff., 178, 179

Walker, John, 120
Walsingham, Sir Francis, 119, 120, 121,
123, 141, 146, 151, 152
Wanchese, 140, 145, 147
Warbeck, Perkin, 25
Warde, Richard, 28
Watts, John, 169, 172, 179
Wentworth, Peter, 110
West Country, 86, 88, 99, 115, 140, 147
West Indies, 14, 44, 45, 46, 48, 74, 89,
90, 97, 98, 103, 114, 116, 122, 145,
149, 150, 151, 152, 159, 163, 166, 169,
171, 172, 180
White, John, 118, 137, 139, 146, 150,
151, 155, 157, 161, 162, 165, 166, 167,
168, 169, 170, 171, 172
Willes, Richard, 119
Willoughby, 48, 55, 101
Wingina, Chief, 138, 151, 156, 158, 163
Wolsey, 33
Wyatt, 101

Zeeland, 83